MYTHS TO LIVE BY

A SKELETON KEY STUDY GUIDE

by

CATHERINE SVEHLA, PhD

JOSEPH CAMPBELL
FOUNDATION

ISBN: 978-1-61178-038-3

Front cover image detail from *Earthrise* by NASA.
Book design by *the*BookDesigners.

First printing edition 2023

www.jcf.org

MYTHS TO LIVE BY

A SKELETON KEY STUDY GUIDE

CONTENTS

The Collected Works of Joseph Campbell

AND THE JOSEPH CAMPBELL FOUNDATION
SKELETON KEY STUDY GUIDE SERIES

At his death in 1987, Joseph Campbell left a significant body of published work that explored his lifelong passion for myths and symbols from many cultures. He also left a large volume of unreleased work: uncollected articles, notes, letters, and diaries, as well as audio and videotape recorded lectures.

The Joseph Campbell Foundation was founded in 1991 to preserve, promote, and perpetuate Campbell's work. The Foundation has undertaken to archive his papers and recordings in digital format, and to publish previously unavailable material and out-of-print works as *The Collected Works of Joseph Campbell*.

The Foundation is now also publishing this series of Skeleton Key Study Guides to accompany selected titles in the *Collected Works*. We intend study guides such as this one to provide entry points into Campbell's ideas for students and for others new to Campbell studies. We hope that Campbell's work and his way of working inspire you to bring new creativity, mythic awareness, and psychological depth to your own work, as they have already done for so many.

How to Use This Study Guide

A skeleton key can open many locks because it has been filed down to only the essentials. This study guide opens *Myths to Live By* the same way. Each chapter of the study guide focuses on a corresponding chapter in *Myths to Live By*. In each chapter, you'll find a summary of the *Myths to Live By* chapter, section by section, followed by points of interest in that chapter as well as complementary reading and audio lists. Chapters close with a selection of discussion questions and prompts for creative projects. Our vision is that this Skeleton Key Study Guide unlocks *Myths to Live By* for you, whether you are new to the material or deepening your relationship with it.

CITATIONS FROM *MYTHS TO LIVE BY*

Whenever this Skeleton Key Study Guide quotes directly from *Myths to Live By*, the text includes footnotes that contain page numbers on which you can find the original citation. These page numbers refer to the edition first published in 1972 by Viking Press, and more recently printed by Penguin Compass.

Campbell, Joseph. *Myths to Live By*. Penguin Compass, 1993.

SKELETON KEY STUDY GUIDE
INTRODUCTION

BY CATHERINE SVEHLA, PHD

"What is—or what is to be—the new mythology?"[1]

In *Myths to Live By,* Joseph Campbell considers the problems and promise contained in this question.

Like millions of other people, I was introduced to Campbell and his work in 1988, when I watched the *Power of Myth* interviews conducted by Bill Moyers. Campbell's passion for myth was electrifying. His insights freed me from myths that didn't fit my understanding and experience of the world. He explained so much! More importantly, Campbell's enthusiasm inspired me to begin my own search for a new myth to live by.

According to Campbell, our biggest challenge and opportunity is the creation of a global community. The world is getting smaller. Technology is dissolving old boundaries between people. In the past, you only knew the myths of your own society. Those myths were an important part of your identity, and you may have been called to defend them. Now we have global travel, the internet, and more diverse communities in many parts of the world. You can learn from different cultures and study their mythologies. For the first time in human history, Campbell explains, we can appreciate the richness of the human imagination *and* understand the common themes of human experience. We can revel in the diversity of our symbols and myths, and come together around a shared vision of human potential. If we use our mythologies correctly, they can move us forward into a new world.

Campbell sees two major obstacles that we need to overcome, in order for this to happen. He talks about both of these problems in *Myths to Live By*. One is the general lack of understanding about the need for myth. Another is the widespread confusion about how to properly read our myths. Mythology, as Campbell explains, is a kind of map of human psychology. Myths are a symbolic description of our inner world and inner journey. Despite their apparent differences, myths from all cultures speak to our shared aspirations, challenges, and desire for awakening. This is why we need these ancient stories. But to understand the message, we must read them as metaphors, not literal facts or history.

In *Myths to Live By*, Campbell draws on his scholarship and storytelling ability to address these themes from many perspectives. He discusses archeology, theology, the arts, and science. He offers an in-depth comparison of Eastern and Western mythological traditions. He draws on a range of cultures to explore mythologies of love and war. He talks about LSD, schizophrenia, and shamanism, and examines the mythological images that link these different experiences. Seen through Campbell's insightful lens, the problems created by our misunderstanding of mythology are clear. So are the solutions that he offers, and the exciting possibilities.

My personal and professional devotion to mythology has taken decades to mature. I've studied art and architecture, Buddhism and earth-based religious practices, somatic therapies and depth psychology. In 2008, I earned a PhD in Mythological Studies with an emphasis in Depth Psychology from Pacifica Graduate Institute. Then I began my current work as an independent scholar, teacher, and storyteller. I still marvel at the incredible usefulness of Campbell's ideas in my everyday life. I am still inspired by the example of his life and work, and his spirit of adventure.

Myths to Live By is a wide-ranging exploration of many of Campbell's important ideas. It is based on a dozen lectures that he presented at the Cooper Union for the Advancement of Science and Art in New York City between 1958 and 1971. This was a turbulent time in the United States and around the world. These political and cultural changes are still unfolding today. Our myths are an important part of the puzzle, Campbell explains. They can either hold us back or help us move forward into new and exciting possibilities.

Myths to Live By is a provocative book. You might not agree with Campbell on every point. He is critical of the old myths— Western mythologies in particular—in today's world. He has strong opinions about twentieth-century American culture. In addition, some social conventions and language have changed since this book was written. Campbell uses gendered words like "mankind," for example. Some of his terminology, words like "primitive," "Oriental," "East," and "West," have been redefined or replaced in common usage. If you find Campbell challenging, make this an opportunity to reflect. What do these cultural shifts mean to you? To your mythology? Take Campbell's work as an invitation to think critically about important questions that shape your life.

If you would like to learn more about Campbell's life, I recommend the biography *Joseph Campbell: A Fire in the Mind*, by Stephen and Robin Larsen. I also suggest that you read *The Hero's Journey: Joseph Campbell on His Life and Work*. This book is a series of interviews with Campbell, conducted by a number of his most interesting colleagues, and is part of *The Collected Works of Joseph Campbell* published by the Joseph Campbell Foundation.

Myths to Live By is a valuable starting point for an exploration of Campbell's work and of mythology in general. Because the book originated as a lecture series, each chapter stands on its own as a complete investigation of a specific topic. That said, sequential reading might be best if Campbell's work is new to you. At the end of each chapter of this study guide you will find a suggested reading list of works by Campbell and others. I've also listed the titles of some of Campbell's audio lectures, which are available on the Joseph Campbell Foundation website. These resources may help you dive into specific topics that interest you. There is also a short list of questions to help you reflect on the topics and themes discussed in that chapter.

What is, or will be, the new mythology? Campbell uses the metaphor of "no horizons" to express his vision of the future and the new mythology. "No horizons" describes a global community dedicated to the development of all human potential. It describes a mythology that brings us together and ends the tribal conflicts that have separated us for thousands of years. Do you have a vision of a new mythology? What does a "myth to live by" mean to you? With Campbell as your guide and conversation partner, you are certain to find new answers to these questions. I hope you find this guide useful and enjoy the adventure as much as I do.

NOTES

1 Campbell, *Myths to Live By*, 250.

Chapter 1
The Impact of Science on Myth

Chapter Summary

Campbell begins this chapter with a humorous anecdote about a conversation he overheard between a little boy and his mother at a lunch counter. They disagreed about the origins of our species. Were Adam and Eve the "first parents" of humankind? Or does science offer a more accurate theory? Mom insisted that the Bible was the truth. The little boy replied that the scientists had the facts, and the bones. Which one of them is right?

The scientific world view has raised challenging questions about the validity of mythology today. Many people believe that a society with modern science doesn't need myth. In this chapter, Campbell looks at the centuries-long conflict between science and mythology (or religion). It is possible both to accept scientific facts and to have a myth to live by, Campbell says. Science and mythology can support each other. In fact, they must support each other if we want to develop our full human potential. How is this accomplished?

As Campbell explains, science and mythology meet different needs. Science, he says, is a never-ending investigation of the outer world. Science generates factual information about the physical world. We need this information to survive and thrive. We need this information to satisfy our curiosity and to live with greater comfort and security. Because science is fact-based, the "truth" in scientific information is literal. It also changes. The "true" or reliable facts of science today may be different tomorrow, because science is the art of experimenting. Science is the work of testing out theories and exploring uncharted territory. When new facts are discovered, our literal understanding of the material world changes.

Mythology is the story of our inner life, told through symbols and metaphors. Our myths describe the psychological and spiritual journey of life. They help us make meaning of the material world. They offer answers to questions like "why am I here?" Mythological "truth" is metaphorical. The outer form of a myth may change. Old symbols may lose their meaning and need to be replaced. But the essential realizations in myth don't change, because the core challenges and questions of human existence are constant. We are born, develop an identity and place in the world, and die. The myths or religions of different cultures seem very different and yet, according to Campbell, the metaphors all point to the same fundamental, unchanging truths. In *The Hero with a Thousand Faces*, Campbell outlined this "monomyth" as the "hero's journey." Aldous Huxley called it "the perennial philosophy."

According to Campbell, there have been times when the scientific and mythological view of the world were essentially the same. In the Middle Ages, for example, people thought that the earth was a stationary sphere in the center of the solar system. Some thought that the earth was flat. This model was based on the best science at the time, inherited from the ancient Greeks. It was also the teaching of the Christian church. There was a common understanding that God's laws ruled the cosmos on the material and spiritual planes. There is a short discussion of this harmonious model below, in the Points of Interest section.

"They are telling us in picture language of powers of the psyche to be recognized and integrated into our lives, powers... which represent that wisdom of the species by which man has weathered millenniums."

—MYTHS TO LIVE BY, *page 14*

Then early European explorers, like Columbus and Magellan, discovered that the earth is not flat. Early astronomers, like Copernicus and Galileo, discovered that the earth is not the center of the solar system, and that it moves around the sun. The loss of certainty about these basic facts shook European culture. The accepted model of a divine order began to crumble. As the centuries passed, a battle for the "truth" began. Over time, science and mythology diverged.

The struggle continues, Campbell explains, because many people are confused about the difference between science and myth. They take both scientific facts and mythology literally. They think they must choose between them, like the little boy and his mother at the lunch counter. This slows down scientific progress. It also undermines our understanding of the purpose of mythology and mythological truth, because we don't understand the metaphors.

Historically, people who chose science denied the need for myth because it is not factual. They cut themselves off from their inner life and failed to see the role myth plays in their lives. On the other hand, Christian authorities have often tried to argue that the Bible is a factual, historical record of creation and human life on earth, despite scientific discoveries, archeological evidence, and religious scholarship. According to Campbell, they have forgotten that myth is a metaphorical and symbolic description of the inner life, of human psychology and spiritual aspirations. By insisting that people believe that Biblical events actually happened as recorded, they have exchanged the profound truth contained in the mythic symbols for something absurd.

12

This disconnect between science and myth causes great instability, Campbell explains. We've seen this trouble many times, as colonizing cultures destroyed the mythologies of indigenous societies. People lost their sense of meaning and direction. These cultures fell apart, he says, and the whole way of life collapsed. Some colonizers thought they were paving the way for a better, more scientific world. Others thought that they were bringing the only true religion, Christianity, to misguided or savage people. Both brought disaster. Now the descendants of the colonizers are having a similar experience themselves.

How can the disconnect between science and myth be repaired? Mythology, Campbell says, reveals the "facts of the mind." These are the universal themes, symbols, and mythic figures found in the myths of all cultures. Campbell names two fields that study the facts of the mind: comparative mythology and psychology. Depth psychology and the work of C.G. Jung, in particular, could be very useful. Jung balanced a scientific approach to psychology with a deep appreciation for the inner life, Campbell explains. Jung analyzed psychological phenomena and found the mythological roots. This type of psychology, Campbell says, could deepen our knowledge of our inner journey through life and also help us live in the factual, outer world without conflict between the two.

According to Campbell, we need both science and mythology to realize our full potential, and these two paradigms must be compatible. To achieve this, we have to recognize the different roles that science and myth play in our lives. We have to accept scientific information as literal fact and interpret our myths metaphorically. We also have to be willing to let both forms of knowledge change. Life is a mystery, he observes. Science has

"For the really great and essential fact about the scientific revelation—the most wonderful and most challenging fact—is that science does not and cannot pretend to be 'true' in any absolute sense."

—MYTHS TO LIVE BY, *page 14*

transformed the world and will continue to push the boundaries. Who knows what we might discover about the outer world or our own consciousness, if we approach the adventure of life with an open mind?

There is a lot of uncertainty today, Campbell says, and this is difficult. New possibilities can be inspiring and frightening at the same time. He concludes this lecture with a story from Hindu mythology: The gods and their archenemies, the demons, decide to work together to churn the Milky Ocean and bring up the butter of immortality. This is hard work and it takes a long time. A cloud of poison rises from the ocean and threatens to kill them all. Then the god Shiva, the lord of life, death, and creation, swallows the poisonous cloud. It turns his throat blue but he contains the poison. At long last, the butter, the sun and moon, and other essential gifts are produced. Reconciling the long-standing division between science and mythology is hard work, Campbell suggests, but the rewards will be great.

POINTS OF INTEREST

The resistance to scientific discoveries in the Middle Ages, especially on the part of the Christian church, might be hard to understand. But there was a deep sense of continuity, sacred order, and belonging in the old mythic image of the earth at the center of the cosmos. Nothing in contemporary cultures that derive from Enlightenment Europe provide this for all of us today, which is part of Campbell's message.

This comforting sense of sacred order was rooted in the philosophy and science of the ancient Greeks. The Greeks observed the seven visible "planets": the moon, Mercury, Venus, the sun, Mars, Jupiter, and Saturn. Each of these represented a particular spiritual energy or power. The Greeks constructed a system of seven days of the week based on the names and energies of the planets. They linked each planet to one of seven notes of the musical scale, and to a specific metal, like silver or copper. This was called "the celestial harmony." Early Christians lived in this Greek worldview and the Christian church developed within it. They aligned the laws and myth of their new God with the Greek model.

By the Middle Ages, Christians believed that God had established this harmonious cosmic order and reigned in heaven on the outskirts of this solar system. His representatives on earth—the pope and the emperor or king—governed according to this order. Further, every human soul was part of it. Obeying God's law and his representatives was one form of belonging, but the connection went deeper. People thought that a human soul descended from heaven to be born on earth. During this descent, the soul picked up qualities of each of the planets and their associated elements. When you died, your soul returned to heaven. On the way back up, you returned the elements that you had collected for your earthly life to the seven celestial bodies.

As Campbell says, in those days our bodies and souls were made of the same stuff as the cosmos, and sang the same cosmic song. Today, science describes this underlying cosmic unity through the perpetual motion of subatomic particles. The earlier belief that humans are part of an all-encompassing cosmic order has a new basis. We are made of stardust.

COMPLEMENTARY READING FROM CAMPBELL'S WORK

Campbell, Joseph. *The Hero's Journey: Joseph Campbell on His Life and Work.* Edited by Phil Cousineau. New World Library, 2014. *The Collected Works of Joseph Campbell.*

—. *The Power of Myth with Bill Moyers.* With Bill Moyers. Edited by Betty Sue Flowers. Doubleday, 1988.

AUDIO RECORDINGS OF CAMPBELL LECTURES

Campbell, Joseph. "New Horizons." Audio Lecture I.1.4. *The Collected Works of Joseph Campbell.*

—. "Interpreting Symbolic Forms." Audio Lecture I.5.1. *The Collected Works of Joseph Campbell.*

FURTHER READING

Gould, Stephen J. *Wonderful Life: The Burgess Shale and the Nature of History.* Penguin, 1989.

King, Barbara J. *Evolving God: A Provocative View on the Origins of Religion.* Expanded Edition. University of Chicago Press, 2017.

Livio, Mario. *Galileo and the Science Deniers.* Simon and Schuster, 2020.

DISCUSSION QUESTIONS

- How does science shape your view of the world? How does mythology shape your view of the world?

- What do you think of Campbell's explanation of the difference between science and myth? Does his perspective make it possible for you to hold both views?

- Do you think that a society without myth lacks meaning and stability? Why or why not? What can go wrong in a society that rejects science?

CREATIVE PROMPTS

- Write a story that expresses your view of the cosmos.

- Make a collage of the earth as you experience it.

- Come up with your version of the celestial harmony. Assign colors, new names, and pop songs to each of the planets.

CHAPTER 2
THE EMERGENCE OF MANKIND

CHAPTER SUMMARY

PART 1

Why do we need mythology at this point in human history? In Chapter 1, Campbell said that myths are essential to our inner life. Now he explains this in more detail. Evidence suggests that the human species has always made myths, he says, and that we organize our lives around our myths. This distinguishes us psychologically from other animals. He talks about three factors that shape our myth-making. The first and most important is our conscious awareness of death. Death is a troubling part of our psychological reality, he explains. We know that we're going to die and that everyone we love is going to die. Our myths must tell us how to face death.

Second is the realization that you are part of an enduring social order. Your community will continue to exist after you die. Every group finds a successful way of life in their particular environment. This information is carried in myth. Our myths tell us the right way to live as part of society. Different cultures have developed a wide variety of lifestyles, Campbell says, and different ways to meet death.

Finally, every person and every social group has a relationship to the natural world and the universe. We live within the regular life cycles of the earth and the movement of the sun, moon, and other celestial bodies. This is the source, support, and context for life. Every culture weaves an understanding of the natural world into its myths as well.

People live in a wide variety of environments and cultural conditions, with different myths. In the past, Campbell says, different cultural groups had relatively little contact with each other. They could easily live within their own mythology. Today, globalization brings different cultures into greater contact. As Campbell explained in Chapter 1, we must appreciate our differences and embrace our common humanity. Our myths are unique and at the same time they reveal shared themes of the human imagination and experience. Human psychology has fundamental similarities all around the world.

Today's world is different from the old in another important way. In more traditional societies, Campbell explains, myths reinforce the singular value of the community. Members of the group prioritize the stability of community and protect it. Now, Campbell says, our social rules are changing. We care more about individuals and individuality. More and more people prioritize their individual lives over the stability of society. They might take the social order for granted. This will have important implications for mythology, old and new.

PART 2

In Part 2 of this chapter, Campbell examines two myths that offer a path to eternal life: the Christian myth about Adam and Eve in the Garden of Eden, and the Buddhist myth of the Buddha's enlightenment. If you try to read these myths as history, Campbell says, they appear very different. You also miss the real message.

"This recognition of mortality and the requirement to transcend it is the first great impulse to mythology."

—MYTHS TO LIVE BY, *page 22*

A myth describes our "inward spiritual state,"[1] he explains, using images and metaphors. Both of these mythic narratives use the metaphors of a tree of immortal life, a serpent god, and guardians that bar the way to the tree. Campbell elegantly unpacks both of these myths and their symbols to reveal the central spiritual truth: the mystery is within you. The eternal is present in life.

According to Campbell, the difference in traditional perspectives between Asia and Europe is significant. He delves more deeply into the difference in Chapter 5. But the images of a sacred tree and a serpent god are even older than Christianity or Buddhism, as is this spiritual understanding. They can be found in Sumerian mythology and likely go back much further. Given the age of these repeated mythic forms, he says, it's likely that some members of our species have known this from the start.

PART 3

On this intriguing note, Campbell begins Part 3 of this discussion. He shares evidence of our earliest myth-making, from the early human Pithecanthropus, to Neanderthals, to *Homo sapiens.* This part of the chapter centers around early veneration of cave bears, fire, cave paintings, and figurines. In our early days, he observes, other animals were central to our lives. We lived among them and hunted them, and some of them were dangerous. How did the myths of these early hunting groups address death, and our need to kill other living things, especially animals, for food? We can't be certain about archeological evidence, Campbell says, and yet the myths of contemporary indigenous people provide clues.

Campbell talks about the bear cult of the Ainu people in Japan and tells one of their myths. He also tells the North American

Blackfoot myth of the buffalo, and a Polynesian myth about the origin of the coconut tree. These myths describe a pact between humans and animals or plants, and between the spiritual and material realms. According to Campbell, what you find in indigenous mythologies is the belief that there is really no death, because life and death are part of the same cycle. The body dies and the spirit will return. Hunted animals are willing victims, as long as the proper ceremonies are maintained. I take a closer look at Campbell's explanation of the "willing victim" under Points of Interest. He also notes that the female body is inherently mythic as the source of life. In each of the three myths that Campbell discusses, a young woman makes the sacred pact or accepts the gift from the spirit realm, on behalf of her people. Males must be initiated into the power of the mythic realms.

POINTS OF INTEREST

The image of a "willing victim" describes a sacred pact between human beings and animals, and between the material and spiritual realms. In both cases, a cyclical exchange maintains life. Every living thing needs food and is food. Every living thing dies. This shared fate creates a sense of relationship and kinship. A body also has a spirit and connection to the spirit realm. We all move back and forth between the material and spiritual realms, over and over again. Death is the transition. We emerge from the mystery and return to it. According to the myths, humans play a special role in this cycle. They have the prayers, songs, and rituals to keep it going.

In some cultures, the image of the "willing victim" included plants and even human beings, who offered their lives to preserve

*"They speak, therefore,
not of outside events but of
themes of the imagination."*

—MYTHS TO LIVE BY, *page 26*

the fertility of the world. Campbell ends this chapter with a Polynesian myth about a maiden and a mysterious shape-shifting eel. The eel's willing self-sacrifice resulted in the coconut tree, a source of food to this day. Campbell talks more about mythologies in which humans were the "willing victims" in Chapter 4.

COMPLEMENTARY READING FROM CAMPBELL'S WORK

Campbell, Joseph. *The Masks of God, Volume 1: Primitive Mythology.* Edited by David Kudler. New World Library, 2020. *The Collected Works of Joseph Campbell.*

AUDIO RECORDINGS OF CAMPBELL LECTURES

Campbell, Joseph. "The Celebration of Life." Audio Lecture I.1.1. *The Collected Works of Joseph Campbell.*

—. "The Religious Impulse." Audio Lecture I.5.5. *The Collected Works of Joseph Campbell.*

FURTHER READING

Armstrong, Karen. *Short History of Myth.* Canongate Books, 2005.

Eliade, Mircea. *The Myth of the Eternal Return: Cosmos and History.* Translator Willard R. Trask. Introduction by Jonathan Z. Smith. Princeton University Press; reprint edition, 2018.

Grinnell, George Bird. *Blackfeet Indian Stories.* Riverbend Publishing, 2005.

Discussion Questions

- What is your perspective on death? Is this rooted in a mythology or symbols like Christ or Buddha? Where did your idea of death come from?

- Campbell says that you can live your daily life with a sense of the eternal. What do you think? What does this mean to you?

- What do you think about the idea of a "willing victim"? Does it change your perspective on food?

- What did you learn from this chapter that surprised you or feels significant?

Creative Prompts

- Write a poem about death or about the death of someone or something you loved.

- We all have rituals or routines around our morning coffee or tea, and our mealtimes. Notice what you do at these times and experiment with small ways to make these daily events more meaningful.

NOTES

1 Campbell, *Myths to Live By*, 27.

CHAPTER 3
THE IMPORTANCE OF RITES

CHAPTER SUMMARY

Campbell now provides another reason that we need myth: to provide the forms that define our lives. Every living thing expresses the instincts and patterns of behavior unique to its species, he says. Other animals are born knowing most of the behaviors that they need to survive but humans are different. We have a lot to learn in order to survive and be part of a family and community. Campbell calls this necessary shaping and teaching "imprinting." Imprinting is done through our myths. According to Campbell, rites or rituals are a powerful form of mythic imprinting.

Humans are also different from other animals in another way. We take a long time to mature and become self-sufficient. Most mammals, Campbell observes, can leave their parents and live on their own within weeks, even days or hours, after birth. A human being is dependent on other people for much longer. In a sense, a person must be born twice. The first birth is physical, as a dependent baby who comes into the world. The second birth is psychological, as a self-responsible adult who takes a place in society. Rituals are an important part of these transitions, especially the second birth, and yet many modern people don't receive this guidance anymore.

In traditional societies and times past, young people were ritually initiated into their assigned roles in the community. Today, many of us grow up without a meaningful rite of passage. We can stay in a dependent state for too long. This is a problem for the individual and for the society, Campbell says, and yet what works in traditional cultures is not the solution in modern industrialized societies. Today, many of us grow up with the idea of personal freedom. We are expected to learn to think for ourselves and take personal responsibility. We are expected to innovate and contribute to the creation of society. We want to live our unique, chosen life, not be an obedient cog in a relatively stagnant social order. This notion of the individual is central to the human potential Campbell envisions. The concept of the individual is a primary theme in the next few chapters.

Unfortunately, Campbell observes, this idea of personal freedom can lead to a lack of appreciation for social conditioning and cultural forms. Some people champion the "natural" human, as if culture is a uniformly bad influence. This leads to degradation of society and the individual. We live in the matrix of myth and mythic forms. We need the bridge they provide, between the consciousness of the everyday material world and the unconscious. We need the inner life. We need the structures and rituals, the roles and the rules. We find our personal expression through mastering and refining the forms, perhaps moving beyond them.

There is a form or pattern for everything that we do. Campbell reminds us that art is a potent cultural form. Art is the creative edge of a culture. He describes the Japanese tea ceremony, a dynamic balance between form and spontaneity. The protocol of the ceremony is precise and yet the individual style of the tea master is expressed. The same can be said of athletics, he says. Through learning the rules and developing your skill, you discover your talent.

"The function of ritual, as I understand it, is to give form to human life, not in the way of a mere surface arrangement, but in depth."

—MYTHS TO LIVE BY, *page 44*

Appreciation for ritual may have diminished in modern culture, but we are still deeply affected by ritual forms. Campbell describes his experience of the public mourning for President John F. Kennedy. He explores the mythological roots of the seven gray horses with blackened hooves, the empty saddle, and the flag-draped coffin. A rite like this brings a community together in a powerful way, he says. People might not know the myths. They might not know the meaning behind the symbols but the power is felt. Myth and ritual speak to our imagination. They satisfy an instinctual need in human consciousness.

The real question, then, is what inspires us today? What inspires the awe that gives rise to mythologies, and the forms that support vibrant societies and individuals? In the past, we found this in our fellow animals, in the life cycle of plants, and in the movement of the celestial bodies. Then the ancient Greeks suggested that man himself was the great embodiment of the mystery. The human being is a microcosm of the cosmos. Humanism has been a powerful idea throughout European history. Campbell ends on a suggestive note, with Robinson Jeffers's poem "Natural Music." The medium is part of Campbell's message, because a poem is a cultural form. The poem contains a call for humans to rejoin the natural world and its mystery.

Points of Interest

In this chapter, Campbell explains our need for cultural forms and their source in our myths. These forms operate in our lives on four levels, which correspond to Campbell's definition of the four functions of myth: Myth connects us to the mysteries

MYTHS TO LIVE BY: A SKELETON KEY STUDY GUIDE

of life and experiences of awe and wonder. This is the *mystical* function. Myth also provides our image of the cosmic order. This is the *cosmological* function.

The cosmological function of myth gives rise to the *sociological* function. People create the forms that define and organize their society. Finally, the myths and forms guide an individual through all of the phases of life, from birth to death. This is the *pedagogical*, or teaching function of myth.

Although Campbell doesn't devote one lecture or chapter to this topic, the four functions of myth appear over and over again in *Myths to Live By*. He outlines them in Chapter 10, "Schizophrenia—The Inward Journey." They are central to his perspective on mythology and its value for us today. I find it useful to keep these four functions in mind as I read *Myths to Live By*.

COMPLEMENTARY READING FROM CAMPBELL'S WORK

Campbell, Joseph, and Henry Morton Robinson. *A Skeleton Key to Finnegans Wake: Unlocking James Joyce's Masterwork.* Foreword and updates by Edmund L. Epstein. New World Library, 2013. *The Collected Works of Joseph Campbell.*

—. *Thou Art That: Transforming Religious Metaphor.* Edited and with foreword by Eugene Kennedy, PhD. New World Library, 2001. *The Collected Works of Joseph Campbell.*

"Myths are the mental support of rites; rites the physical enactment of myths."

—MYTHS TO LIVE BY, *page 45*

"We have, consequently, the comparatively complex problem in educating our young of training them not simply to assume uncritically the patterns of the past, but to recognize and cultivate their own creative possibilities; not to remain on some proven level of biology and sociology, but to represent a movement of the species forward."

—MYTHS TO LIVE BY, *page 48*

AUDIO RECORDINGS OF CAMPBELL LECTURES

Campbell, Joseph. "The Necessity of Rites." Audio Lecture I.4.4. *The Collected Works of Joseph Campbell.*

FURTHER READING

Driver, Tom F. *Liberating Rites: Understanding the Transformative Power of Rituals.* Westview Press, 1998.

Frobenius, Leo, and Douglas C. Fox. *African Genesis.* B. Blom, 1966.

Okakuru, Kazuko. *The Book of Tea.* Kodansha International, 1989.

Some, Malidoma Patrice. *Ritual: Power, Healing and Community.* First edition. Penguin Books, 1997.

Joyce, James. *Portrait of the Artist as a Young Man* (Wordsworth Classics). Revised edition. Wordsworth Editions Ltd., 1997

DISCUSSION QUESTIONS

- Which rituals and ceremonies have shaped your life? Did they inspire awe? Why or why not?

- Have you ever had an experience of profound awe or wonder? Could a rite be created from it?

- High school graduations and Fourth of July fireworks are two examples of secular (non-religious) rituals. Can you come up with a list of other examples? What do these community rituals say about the values of the community?

- Can you trace the history of any of these secular rituals to find a possible mythological origin?

- If myths are the source of our cultural forms, how does social change take place? What are the implications of this, for people who want to impact their society in some way?

- Do you agree that personal freedom and expression is found through mastering the rules and forms? Why or why not?

CREATIVE PROMPTS

- Write a description of a typical wedding ceremony in your culture, as if you were an anthropologist or a mythologist observing the event.

- Go through the daily news and make a list of the shared rituals taking place. Include activities that we don't commonly see as rituals, like watching a football game or going to the movies.

- Write a short story about a personal initiation that you've undergone. What happened? What did you learn?

Chapter 4

The Separation of East and West

Chapter Summary

PART 1

You might take our contemporary concept of the word "individual" for granted. Your personal freedom might seem so obvious and natural that you don't consider a world without it. But most people have lived in societies that had no place for "individuality." It wasn't natural or useful. It wasn't part of their myths. As Campbell explains, the European concept of the "individual" is a tremendous realization. He calls it a "properly human spiritual ideal, true to the highest potentiality of our species."[1] An individual with self-awareness and free will brings something new and valuable into the world.

In this chapter, Campbell discusses the evolution of individuality in Europe. He highlights the significance of this concept through a comparison between Asian and European ideas. Campbell continues this comparison in the next two chapters. Throughout these discussions, he defines the "East" as India, China, and Japan, and the "West" as the Levant (Middle East) and Europe. Each of these geographical and cultural domains has a distinct character, history, and global influence. Each of them has a different mythology.

First Campbell sets the stage. As he explained in the previous chapters, our forms of social organization come from our myths, and the mythic image of the natural order they provide.

Human beings first found their mythic inspiration in animals and plants, then in the movements of the planets and stars. Their myths taught them to harmonize with natural cycles. Their social structures mirrored the order they observed in nature. Everyone and everything had a purpose and role to play in the cycle of life. This central idea persisted as our social structures changed from bands of hunter-gatherers, to farmers, to citizens in growing city-states. Society was a microcosm of the cosmic order.

Then life in the ancient cities got more complex. Now there were farmers, craftspeople, priests, traders, kings, and merchants. Each had a specific role to play. The cosmic laws were called the *Me* (Sumerian), *Maat* (Egyptian), *Tao* (Chinese), or *Dharma* (Sanskrit). From these mythic viewpoints, there was no individual life or personal meaning. This was true for every member of the community. Campbell talks about the ritual sacrifice of kings and their entire court, including the animals. Today the idea of human sacrifice is gruesome and yet, as Campbell observes, there might have been something noble about identifying with the great cosmic drama. In living your role, you were a meaningful part of the eternal whole.

PART 2

In Part 2, Campbell compares the European "individual" to Asian ideas. The key difference between East and West in this context, he says, is the importance placed on the roles that we play in life. In Asian mythologies, the individual is in service to the cosmic order. There is no meaningful identity beyond the roles you play. They are determined by karma, the cosmic law.

"To become—in Jung's terms— individuated, to live as a released individual, one has to know how and when to put on and to put off the masks of one's various life roles."

—MYTHS TO LIVE BY, *page 67*

The goal is to be egoless, to achieve release from the wheel of reincarnation. To be attached to something as transitory as your personality in this lifetime is only a hindrance.

In European myth, a person also plays social roles. You might be "mother," "son," "artist," "brother," "wife," "truck driver," or "neighbor," for example, but these are not your whole self. These roles are essential to our social organization and to our sense of identity. The highest value is placed on the individual, not the role. You are expected to know yourself, develop your individuality, and know how "to be yourself" in the right situations. C.G. Jung called our social roles "personas." They are like masks that we put on and take off. See the Points of Interest section below for more discussion of the Jungian ideas that Campbell uses in this chapter.

According to Campbell, Asian mythologies today reflect the ancient notions of cosmic order. How did change occur in Europe? In part 3, Campbell describes an important shift that began in Mesopotamia around 2000 BCE. The "gods" left the natural world. Divinity receded into the great beyond. Campbell calls this "mythic dissociation." It's characteristic of Judaism, Christianity, and Islam, the mythologies that later developed in the Levant.

Mythic dissociation didn't take place in Asian civilizations. Due to geographic factors like mountain ranges, Asia and Europe continued in relative isolation from each other. Asia retained the old mythic form of the cosmic order. The Middle East and Europe, however, were in constant contact with each other. New ideas spread. They were shared, revised, and shared again. Thus the "separation of East and West," with their distinct mythologies and notions of the individual, individuality, and free will.

The idea that God has left the earth and our material realm has huge implications, Campbell explains. European people lost their intimate connection to the earth as their living source. The material world and human beings were no longer divine. You were no longer part of the eternal cosmic play. God was Other. God was the Creator. These disconnects between the human world, the natural order, and the divine mystery are part of mythic disassociation. Today, many people point to this historical disassociation as the source of our environmental, social, and spiritual crises.

Although much was lost, something was gained. The relocation of the divine ushered in the concept of free will, Campbell says. God now had free will and so did his human creations. In the earlier model of the cosmic order, the gods also played their assigned role. Campbell calls them "cosmic bureaucrats," impersonal functionaries. Now, events took place according to God's will. A natural disaster like the Great Flood, Campbell says, is viewed as a punishment from God, not a regular happening in a long natural cycle. The natural world, human beings, and God are all in relationship with each other. Each of us can choose to be obedient, or not.

Free will, the personal freedom to choose, is essential to the European concept of the individual. In part 4, Campbell emphasizes this point with the aid of three creation myths. In the Indian myth from the Brihadaranyaka Upaniṣad, the Self decides to split itself into male and female and everything else. All is God/Self. In the second chapter of Genesis, God makes man out of dust and woman out of man. God is, and he creates what is not

God. Judaism champions God, Campbell said, because he is the ground of being and created them. So do Christianity and Islam, which both built on this mythological foundation.

In ancient Greek mythology, the gods are not the source. They are created, and they didn't create human beings. The ancient Greeks championed the human being, Campbell says. Humanity was mortal but emerged from the same source as the gods. In Campbell's view, European cultures share the ancient Greek commitment to the individual. Our highest aspiration is the personal fulfillment of our own potential.

Points of Interest

Depth psychology, and the work of C.G. Jung in particular, are essential to understanding Campbell's ideas. Mythology and psychology are closely linked. In Chapter 1, "The Impact of Science on Myth," Campbell refers to Jung's theories about the origins and necessity of myth. Now, Campbell uses depth psychological concepts to explain the European idea of the individual.

In depth psychology, the "ego" is your conscious identity. It is the seat of your personality. You don't want to get rid of the ego. You want to mature through it and become self-aware and self-responsible. This means adequately filling your social roles or "personas" and developing your uniqueness. A psychologically mature person knows the difference between roles and personal identity.

European cultures might say, "there has never been another person like you." The ideal of the individual involves self-awareness

"The aim of individuation requires that one should find and then learn to live out of one's own center, in control of one's for and against."

—MYTHS TO LIVE BY, *page 68*

and development of your unique potential. Jung called this maturation process "individuation." It can be the psychological work of a lifetime. Campbell talks about the inner journey and individuation in Chapter 10.

Complementary Reading from Campbell's Work

Campbell, Joseph. *The Masks of God, Volume 3: Occidental Mythology.* Revised edition. Penguin Books, 1991.

——. *Pathways to Bliss: Mythology and Personal Transformation.* Edited and with foreword by David Kudler. New World Library, 2004. *The Collected Works of Joseph Campbell.*

Audio Recordings of Campbell Lectures

Campbell, Joseph. "Symbolism and the Individual." Audio Lecture I.1.3. *The Collected Works of Joseph Campbell.*

——. "The Individual in Oriental Mythology." Audio Lecture I.1.2. *The Collected Works of Joseph Campbell.*

——. "Hinduism." Audio Lecture I.3.3. *The Collected Works of Joseph Campbell.*

——. "Mythic Living." Audio Lecture I.4.2. *The Collected Works of Joseph Campbell.*

Further Reading

Chiera, Edward. *They Wrote in Clay: The Babylonian Tablets Speak Today*. Edited by George G. Cameron. University of Chicago, 1956.

Jung, C.G. *The Portable Jung*. Edited by Joseph Campbell. Translated by R.F.C Hull. Viking Press, 1971.

Stein, Murray. *Jung's Map of the Soul: An Introduction*. Open Court Books, 1998.

Discussion Questions

• What are the roles that you play in your life? How does this impact your dress, speech, and behavior in certain situations?

• Have you been assigned a role that you wish you played better—or didn't have to play at all? How do you understand your choice?

• According to Campbell, in European cultures the exercise of individual free will is more important than God's will. Do you agree or disagree? Why or why not?

Creative Prompts

• Make a painting or mask that represents your public persona on one side and your private self on the other.

- Look around your house and in your closets. What do your belongings suggest about the various roles that you play? Construct a costume for the "you" that longs to be more visible.

NOTES

1 Campbell, *Myths to Live By*, 61.

CHAPTER 5
THE CONFRONTATION OF
EAST AND WEST IN RELIGION

CHAPTER SUMMARY

Campbell begins with reflections on our shared future. When he was a young man, he thought that reason and science would guide the world to a bright future. He thought the world was through with religion. Then he found the work of Oswald Spengler and Leo Frobenius. These men had a lasting impact on Campbell's thinking. Both of them predict the decline of European cultures. According to Spengler, cultures have a life cycle similar to other living things. They sprout, blossom, and decay. In *The Decline of the West*, Spengler predicts the breakdown of European cultural forms. Leo Frobenius also describes an organic process of cultural development. However, he considered the history of the entire human species. For Spengler, the end of the culture signals dark times ahead. For Frobenius, the decline of the culture means the end of European dominance and the dawn of a more inclusive, creative, global civilization.

The idea that human cultures evolve from simple, "primitive," nonliterate, nontechnological forms to the "more advanced" forms of European civilization is no longer an accepted model. The destructive dominance of Europe, debated by Spengler and Frobenius, is in evidence in these outdated theories. That said, Campbell's response to their arguments is important to us today. History has proven Spengler's predictions, Campbell says. The future of the human race appears uncertain, and yet he shares Frobenius's sense of exciting possibilities. Both men imagine a

"Now, the first and most important effect of a living mythological symbol is to awaken and give guidance to the energies of life."

—MYTHS TO LIVE BY, *page 88*

future of boundless horizons. In this chapter, Campbell points toward a new synthesis of Europe and Asia, and the creative potential in the self-determining individual.

As Campbell explained in the previous chapter, the concept of a self-determining individual is a European idea. It's also revolutionary. The problems we face in living this idea are a primary theme in *Myths to Live By*. In this chapter, he addresses a major problem: the lack of a "living symbol." A "living symbol" is an awe-inspiring mythic image. As discussed in previous chapters, this mythic image defines a culture and a way of life. A living symbol provides meaning and purpose. It connects you to members of your community and to the deeper mystery of life. Christianity used to provide such a symbol, Campbell says. He offers the example of the sacrament of baptism. But Christian belief no longer satisfies all Christians.

Many people are searching for a mythic image that speaks to them. The personal search is an inner search. When the message of outer authorities and religious leaders can't satisfy you, you look into your own heart and mind. Your search is psychological, according to Campbell. You look for self-awareness. You look for direct, personal experience of the mystery, and for your own living symbol. The psychological nature of the search, and the quest for personal experience, make Asian traditions appealing to people whose cultures derive from Europe, Campbell observes. This is what they offer. But there is a problem, which Campbell labels the "confrontation of East and West."

According to Campbell, East and West do not have the same ideas about religion, god, or spiritual practice. This is the "confrontation" between these two cultural domains. The differences aren't easy to reconcile. He explains this with the aid of three personal anecdotes. In each one, there is confusion about the nature of "God" and where or how to look for "him." I've plucked a couple of central ideas from Campbell's personal stories to guide you through his argument.

In European cultures, Campbell says, we've named "God." He's been described in a book from a different time and place. We are supposed to believe that every word of this book is true. We're also supposed to believe that God continues to shape our lives. God is "out there" somewhere and he is our Supreme Creator and Father. We're supposed to have a good relationship with him. Religious practice involves deepening this relationship with God.

In Asia, religious practice is a quest for identity, not relationship. You strive to awaken to the god within, to the eternal aspect of your own being. You are It. The word "Buddha," Campbell explains, means "awakened one." This god is something that you experience, he says. There is nothing to believe in. All of the myths, images, and spiritual practices are designed to help you have a deeper and deeper experience of your consciousness until you awaken to this truth. This identification with "god" is heresy in European religions.

Making the cultural shift from the European religion of relationship to the Asian quest for the inner god is harder than many people realize. These ideas are deeply embedded in our consciousness, even if we aren't religious. So, where can we find a living symbol? Although Campbell takes a dim view of mainstream Christianity, he thinks the images and rites could still be effective. The symbols could offer the possibility of a direct, personal experience of the mystery. This would require reading the myths as metaphor and

abandoning all of the dogma and explanations. Then each person could have their own experience and interpretations. You could discover your own insights and meaning.

Campbell offers a few suggestions about the search for your living symbol, drawn from Asian traditions. He outlines the four yogic paths of Hinduism, which I discuss further in the Points of Interest section. He then turns to the Shinto religion in Japan. The Shinto religion, he says, is a religion of beautiful shrines, images, rituals, music, and dances. There is no scripture or explanation offered. The majesty, beauty, and sensory details of the rites speak for themselves. The point is to experience them with the eyes and heart, to enjoy them. You might be moved to a deep personal experience that is beyond words. You might be transported to a deep state of appreciation for all of life, even the suffering.

In closing, Campbell touches on an important theme, one he returns to many times: To be fully alive, to realize your potential, you need to affirm life, to accept all of it. As the Buddha said, "all life is sorrowful." Trouble will come, so what is your attitude? Campbell tells a Hindu myth of the god Shiva, the goddess Parvati, and the demon Kirttimukha, or "Face of Glory."

This demon is an embodiment of the insatiable hunger that is life, he says. In the story, Shiva watches Kirttimukha eat himself. The demon eats his own body bit by bit until only his face remains. This divine symbol, Campbell writes, expresses the mystery and the horror of life. Life feeds on life. This fundamental truth can't be changed. Any person who seeks to know "god" must accept it.

"Significant images render insights beyond speech, beyond the kinds of meaning speech defines … You don't ask what a dance means, you enjoy it. You don't ask what the world means, you enjoy it. You don't ask what you mean, you enjoy yourself."

—MYTHS TO LIVE BY, *page 102*

Points of Interest

In Hinduism, there are four methods, or yogas, of spiritual practice. As Campbell explains, you are encouraged to adopt the yoga or path that best suits you. All four are effective paths to spiritual awakening.

Jnana yoga is the yoga of knowledge. This is a form of philosophical inquiry that is also a Buddhist practice. Over time, you learn to deconstruct your experience. You stop identifying with your personality, emotions, body, and thoughts in order to find the "witness," the constant point of consciousness. Then you give up the witness too, and become pure consciousness.

Raja yoga, also called "supreme" yoga, is the yoga of meditation, awareness, breath work, and various physical postures and movement. Raja yoga is what non-Indian practitioners commonly call "yoga."

Bhakti yoga is the yoga of devotion to a beloved. You can choose to devote yourself to anyone or anything for whom you feel a deep love, as that love is the presence of the divine within you. Bhakti yoga is the closest to the Christian practice of loving service to God. In India, bhakti yoga requires a guru. You must give up your moral authority and follow the guru. This is difficult for people outside the Hindu culture, Campbells says, and not ideal in his view.

Karma yoga is the yoga of action. This is the teaching that Arjuna receives from the god Krishna in the *Bhagavad Gita*. You must perform the role that you have been assigned in life without any expectations. Do your duty. Everything will die and be reborn no matter what you do. Campbell reminds us that "duty" in India means blind obedience to your social roles. As he discussed in Chapter 4, this definition of duty isn't compatible with the European ideal of a self-responsible adult.

COMPLEMENTARY READING FROM CAMPBELL'S WORK

Campbell, Joseph. *Baksheesh and Brahmin, Asian Journals— India.* Edited by Robin and Stephen Larsen and Antony Van Couvering. New World Library, 2002. *The Collected Works of Joseph Campbell.*

Zimmer, Heinrich. *Myths and Symbols in Indian Art and Civilization.* Edited by Joseph Campbell. Bollingen Series vi. Pantheon, 1946.

AUDIO RECORDINGS OF CAMPBELL'S LECTURES

Campbell, Joseph. "Confrontation of East and West in Religion." Audio Lecture I.2.3. *The Collected Works of Joseph Campbell.*

—. "The World Soul." Audio Lecture I.2.5. *The Collected Works of Joseph Campbell.*

—. "Interpreting Oriental Myth." Audio Lecture I.3.1. *The Collected Works of Joseph Campbell.*

"So, if you really want to help this world, what you will have to teach is how to live in it. And that no one can do who has not himself learned how to live in it in the joyful sorrow and the sorrowful joy of the knowledge of life as it is."

—MYTHS TO LIVE BY, *page 104*

FURTHER READING

Shree Purohit Swami. *The Ten Principal Upanishads.* Contributions from W.B. Yeats. Rupa Publications, 2003.

Easwaran, Eknath. *The Bhagavad Gita.* Second edition. Nilgiri Press, 2007.

Jung, C.G. *Psychology and Religion* (The Terry Lectures Series). Yale University Press, 1960.

Suzuki, Daisetz T. *Zen Buddhism: Selected Writings of D.T. Suzuki.* Edited by William Barrett. Harmony, 1996

DISCUSSION QUESTIONS

- Is there a living mythological symbol or "affect image" in your life? An image that fills you with awe and wonder?

- Consider the difference between "God" as your Creator and "god" as an aspect of your own being. Which of these is most true for you?

- Of the four yogic paths that Campbell outlines, which one do you, or could you, follow as your spiritual path? Or do you see yourself doing something entirely different?

- Campbell says that all societies are ill and the world will always be full of suffering. Do you agree? Why or why not?

CREATIVE PROMPTS

- Write a poem or song that expresses your sense of wonder.

- Pick one of the four yogic paths and write a story about someone who follows it.

- Find or make an image that best represents your notion of the divine.

CHAPTER 6
THE INSPIRATION OF ORIENTAL ART

CHAPTER SUMMARY

In this chapter, Campbell continues his discussion of the search for a living symbol by delving into the topic of Asian, or Oriental, art. He builds on his ideas about the European individual and a new synthesis of Asian and European ideas. European, or "Western" art, Campbell says, reflects an emphasis on individuality and personal expression. In Asia, there is less emphasis on the individual or personal statements. The artist is less expected to innovate. Instead, artistic excellence values the perfection of standard themes. The results can be bland and repetitive, Campbell says, but the best Asian art expresses the presence of the eternal in all things.

Campbell discusses the appropriate subjects and themes of Hindu art in India, and Taoist and Buddhist art in China and Japan. He also explains the spiritual practices that guide the artist. Traditional Asian art is grounded in the symbols and concepts of myth, and the quest for spiritual awakening. Can these images and symbols speak to people in cultures that derive from Europe? Is a cross-cultural art essential to a new mythology? By offering this primer on the spiritual principles of Asian art, Campbell encourages and inspires the exploration of these questions.

Although the purpose of Asian art is spiritual awakening, India has different ways of approaching this task than China and Japan do. As Campbell explains, the Indian artist is a yogi. The artist meditates on an established vocabulary of symbols that

"Listen to any sound or silence at all without interpreting it, and the Anahata will be heard of the Void that is the ground of being, and the world that is the body of being, the Silence and the Syllable."

—MYTHS TO LIVE BY, *page 112*

has been refined for centuries. When a vision appears, the artist renders this image. Art is a spiritual revelation, Campbell says. Symbols of the divine energies of life come through the artist. They depict a transcendent reality and timeless consciousness. If you meditate on the image, as the artist mediated on the theme, you may also be transported to the transcendent reality beyond words or images. Campbell talks at length about the yoga of art, the chakra system, and kundalini. See the Points of Interest section for details.

Hindu art depicts the gods and mythological themes, Campbell says. You find very little daylight reality. In Buddhist and Taoist traditions, art depicts the eternal dimension in the everyday. The primary form is landscapes. The artist takes inspiration from the natural world, called "the world of ten thousand things" (from the Tao Te Ching). Here, the artist's meditation is close observation and deep alignment with the rhythms and textures of the material world. Campbell outlines the six principles of classical painting using the example of an artist painting bamboo. The six principles are rhythm, organic form, trueness to nature, color, placement of the object in the field, and style. By capturing the unique beauty of a bird, blossom, or bit of bamboo, the artist leads the viewer to contemplate the eternal unity that is the source of all things.

This eternal unity is the interaction between yang and yin. As Campbell explains, *yang* and *yin* literally mean the sunny and shady sides of a stream. These two terms contain all of the qualities and forces of the world: light and dark, dry and moist, masculine and feminine, for example. Everything comes into being through the dynamic relationships between yin and yang. The artist, putting black ink on white paper, is wielding the same creative forces that produced the artist, his tools, his understanding, and everything else. In mastering the interplay of yin and yang, the artist plays with the infinite potential of the universe.

Campbell ends by reflecting on the Chinese term *wu wei,* or "not forcing." Things happen spontaneously according to their nature, he says. Let them. The sun rises every morning without your effort. You can let yourself be without effort, too. You take a breath without deciding to do so. Following this principle of nonaction, you let the world unfold. You act spontaneously from the point of stillness in your own center. This is a discipline of unremitting alertness, Campbell says, to the present moment. In alertness, you find aliveness. This is living life as art.

Points of Interest

The Indian chakra system is a series of seven "psychological centers" in the body, from the root to the top of the head, that correspond to the stages of awakening. The movement of spiritual energy up through the chakras is activated by the upward movement of kundalini energy. Kundalini, which is imagined as a great serpent, is a feminine, life-giving force in the body. The purpose of yogic practice is to move your kundalini up through the chakras to the seventh, at the top of your head. The seventh chakra is the seat of spiritual awareness.

Campbell provides a detailed outline of the chakra system. He includes all the primary elements of the iconography. For each chakra, he provides the location in the body, the Sanskrit name and meaning, the specific energy associated with it, and the

"Indian art, that is to say, is an art concerned with the transcendence of our normal two-eyed experience of life, meant to open this third eye, in the middle of the forehead, of the lotus of command [...]."

—MYTHS TO LIVE BY, *page 115*

associated element: water, fire, earth, or air. He also discusses the image of the lotus associated with each chakra. All of these details are part of meditation on each chakra.

Campbell takes special care to unpack the fourth chakra, or heart chakra. The experience of transcendent consciousness, depicted in Indian art, begins here. This consciousness extends through the sixth chakra, the *anja* or mind. The lotus of the fourth chakra is called "Anahata." This is equivalent to the primal energy expressed in the sacred syllable *OM*. Like the chakra system, OM or AUM contains the energetic levels of existence that a person can perceive. Campbell diagrams the four symbolic elements of the syllable: A, U, M, and silence. The silence that surrounds the sound, before and after, is the pure potential that remains when the sound or form has passed away.

COMPLEMENTARY READING FROM CAMPBELL'S WORK

Campbell, Joseph. *Myths of Light: Eastern Metaphors of the Eternal*. Edited by David Kudler. New World Library, 2003. *The Collected Works of Joseph Campbell*.

AUDIO RECORDINGS OF CAMPBELL LECTURES

Campbell, Joseph. "Imagery of Rebirth Yoga." Audio Lecture I.2.4. *The Collected Works of Joseph Campbell*.

—. "Creativity in Oriental Mythology." Audio Lecture I.3.5. *The Collected Works of Joseph Campbell*.

—. "The Sound AUM and Kundalini Yoga." Audio: Lecture II.1.3. *The Collected Works of Joseph Campbell.*

Further Reading

Avalon, Arthur. *The Serpent Power: The Secrets of Tantric and Shaktic Yoga.* Lost Library, 2012.

Coomaraswamy, Ananda K. *The Dance of Siva: Essays on Indian Art and Culture.* Revised edition. Dover Publications, 1985.

Huizinga, Johan. *Homo Ludens: A Study of the Play-Element in Culture.* Martino Fine Books, 2014.

Lao-Tze. *The Canon of Reason and Virtue (Tao Te Ching).* Translated by D.T. Suzuki and Paul Carus. Open Court, 1974.

Discussion Questions

- Have you ever been moved beyond words by an aesthetic experience? What was your experience?

- How has Campbell changed your appreciation for Asian art? What have you learned?

- Is Asian art or art from European cultures more interesting to you? Why?

"Life as an art and art as a game—
as action for its own sake, without
thought of gain or of loss, praise
or blame—is the key, then, to the
turning of living itself into a yoga,
and art into the means to such a life."

—MYTHS TO LIVE BY, *page 124*

CREATIVE PROMPTS

- Experiment with yin and yang by drawing or painting a picture using only black, white, and shades of gray.

- Find images of a Hindu god or goddess. Identify the common characteristics and find out what they symbolize.

- Find a video of someone practicing Tai Chi or Qigong and try out this practice.

CHAPTER 7
ZEN

CHAPTER SUMMARY

In this chapter, Campbell explains the concept and practice of Buddhism and Japanese Zen. Japanese Zen is one of many Buddhist paths to enlightenment, an awakening to the mystery within and without. Zen is a psychological quest for knowledge of the self. Understanding is based in personal experience. There is no god to believe in, or ultimate authority outside the self. This is a huge part of Zen's appeal to Campbell and to many other people as well. You aren't expected to take anyone else's word as truth. You experiment with the method for yourself. Zen could be a valuable part of the synthesis of Asian and European traditions.

Campbell begins by distinguishing two different approaches to Buddhist practice. One is *tariki,* the "way of the kitten." *Tariki* means "outside strength." In this tradition, practitioners petition a mythical Buddha known as Amitabha (Sanskrit) or Amida (Japanese) to grant them release from the cycles of rebirth. Amitabha (or Amida) carries the practitioner, so to speak, the way a mother cat carries her kitten by the scruff of its neck. The other approach is *joriki,* the "way of the monkey." *Joriki* means "own strength." This is the path of self-help, called Mahayana Buddhism in India and Zen in Japan. There are no images or concepts of any gods in Zen. You don't even need the Buddha. You develop a practice and go to work on yourself, similar to the way young monkeys hold onto their mothers with their own strength.

Campbell provides an overview of the history of Zen as it moved from India to China and Japan. He discusses some of the important teachers. He offers a brief summary of key concepts like the Four Noble Truths and the Eight-fold Path. See the Points of Interest section for more information on these concepts. Throughout, Campbell returns to the theme of personal effort.

Along the way, Campbell illustrates his points with many Buddhist stories. This is a central teaching practice in the Buddhist tradition. Stories are the best way to communicate the principles, practices, and purpose of Buddhism, especially Zen Buddhism. When Campbell tells the myth of the Buddha's awakening, he doesn't stop at the moment of enlightenment. He considers the Buddha's dilemma as a teacher. How do you teach something that can't be taught? How do you explain a liberation that can't be described by any except those who have already experienced it?

Buddha developed a basic set of concepts and a method to practice. He taught for over thirty years and left behind many parables and stories. Over the centuries, other Buddhists have built on this foundation. Centuries later, a wealth of information about Buddhist life and practice is available. Still, Campbell says, you have to find the way that works for you. Serious Buddhist practitioners used to think that you had to abandon the world and live in a monastery to succeed. But people have stayed in the world and achieved release. Even the correct definition of concepts like Eight-fold Path has generated debate and disagreement among different Buddhist schools.

This is the last chapter in *Myths to Live By* that is devoted to Asian mythology. Do you have a deeper appreciation for the

"And although each may tend to identify himself mainly with his separate body and its frailties, it is possible also to regard one's body as a mere vehicle of consciousness and to think then of consciousness as the one presence here made manifest through us all."

—MYTHS TO LIVE BY, *page 128*

cultural differences between Asia and cultures derived from Europe? Do you sense exciting possibilities for the future, in the meeting of these two mythological paradigms?

Campbell ends this chapter with an Indian story about a young man who is almost trampled by an elephant after an enlightening moment with his guru. I wonder if he is reminding us to live from both the heart and the head, to find the space between doing and not doing, and the rapture of being alive.

Points of Interest

As Campbell explains, what the Buddha taught was a way to practice, a method or "vehicle" to the enlightenment that he achieved under the bodhi tree. The core teaching is the Four Noble Truths. Campbell briefly explains them but it's difficult to locate all four in the text. Here they are with a few additional notes:

First Noble Truth: All life is sorrowful. No matter what we do, no matter how hard we try to perfect the world, there will always be hardship, illness, death, and the fears and desires of the human ego.

Second Noble Truth: Clinging is suffering. If you can accept the First Noble Truth, then you understand that everything is exactly as it should be, because everything is connected to and causes everything else. This is the Doctrine of Mutual Arising. You can't pull out one thread without unraveling it all. The ego refuses to accept this. The ego has fears and desires, expectations and preferences. These attachments create suffering.

Third Noble Truth: There is release from sorrow. It is possible to understand your ego and the rest of your psychology so deeply that you see right through it and let it go. It is possible to move beyond names, concepts, categories, and meanings, as Campbell says, to a state of simply being. This is the purpose of Buddhist meditation.

Fourth Noble Truth: The release from sorrow is Nirvana. This noble truth is the Eight-fold Path, the Buddhist method. As Campbell explains, the eight aspects of this path are Right Views (or understanding), Right Aspirations (willingness to change), Right Speech (truthful and helpful), Right Conduct (act carefully, don't cause pain), Right Livelihood (don't abuse, exploit, or cause harm while meeting your needs), Right Effort (choose to be happy), Right Meditation (maintain a relaxed attention and focus), and Right Rapture (mindfulness, balance, acceptance of your present experience).

Complementary Reading from Campbell's Work

Campbell, Joseph. *The Masks of God, Volume 2: Oriental Mythology.* Penguin, 1992. *The Collected Works of Joseph Campbell.*

———. *Sake and Satori: Asian Journals.* Edited by David Kudler. New World Library, 2002. *The Collected Works of Joseph Campbell.*

Audio Recordings of Campbell Lectures

"A number of schools of Occidental [European-derived] psychological therapy hold that what we all most need and are seeking is meaning for our lives. For some, this may be a help; but all it helps is the intellect, and when the intellect sets to work on life with its names and categories, recognitions of relationship and definitions of meaning, what is inwardmost is readily lost."

—MYTHS TO LIVE BY, *page 130*

Campbell, Joseph. "Buddhism." Audio Lecture I.3.4. *The Collected Works of Joseph Campbell.*

Further Reading

Herrigel, Eugen. *Zen in the Art of Archery.* Translated by R.F.C. Hull. Vintage Books, 1989.

Kapleau, Roshi Philip. *The Three Pillars of Zen.* 25th anniversary edition. Doubleday, 1989.

Martin, Rafe. *Endless Path, Awakening the Buddhist Imagination: Jataka tales, Zen Practice, and Daily Life.* North Atlantic Books, 2010.

Watts, Alan. *The Way of Zen.* Pantheon, 1957.

Discussion Questions

- Does Zen Buddhism appeal to you? Why or why not? Do you see this type of psychological work as a spiritual practice?

- Are you following the Way of the Kitten or the Way of the Monkey in your life generally?

- What are the strengths and weaknesses of each of these two approaches? Are they both helpful?

- Which aspect of the Eight-fold Path would you find most difficult to practice?

CREATIVE PROMPTS

- Imagine that you are a comparative mythologist and write an article about a new mythology that blends Asian and European traditions. What is the name of this mythology? What are the core values and characteristics? How does this mythology influence the way that people live?

- Write a Zen haiku.

CHAPTER 8
THE MYTHOLOGY OF LOVE

CHAPTER SUMMARY

In this chapter, Campbell reveals love's power to transform us. Seen through Campbell's eyes, mythologies of love are not light-hearted stories of romance, roses, and Cupid. He focuses on the commitment that love requires, and the intensity of the experience. He talks about the agony and challenges that love can bring. He explores the possibility of rapture, a love that dissolves the illusion of separate-ness. Like a moth drawn to a flame, he says, you gladly lose yourself. He suggests, once again, that you have to accept the suffering in the world to be fully alive. He touches on his central theme, the promise of the individual and the quest for self-realization. Love, he explains, can be a path to your true self, to your beloved, to God, and to life. Love can transform you. You can awaken through love.

Campbell invokes mythologies from different cultures to show us the varied faces of love. He offers several examples of gods of love: the ancient Greek Eros, the Hindu god Krishna, and the Christian Christ. He explores the medieval legends of Tristan and Isolt, and Parzival and the Holy Grail. Campbell also weaves in meditations on love from famous works in literature by Dante, William Blake, Sartre, Bernard Shaw, and Thomas Mann. He talks about different forms and types of love. He talks about love that is beyond laws and social convention. Love that is worth every type of suffering. Love that inspires selfless behavior and heroic acts. Love for another person and love for God. Love that unifies. Love as the source of all that exists.

According to Campbell, the power of love has often been misunderstood, especially in Christianity. A distinction is often made between the earthly love of the body and spiritual love. He calls these two types of love passion or *eros*, and compassion or *agape*. Our earthly passion for another person and for the world has been disdained as a "lower" type of love because the body is sinful and the earth is an imperfect place. People believe heavenly perfection is the goal, he explains. In fact, some think that *eros* is in conflict with *agape* and the higher, spiritual love for God. This distinction is false, Campbell says, when you *are* love.

One example of "being" love is the Eastern concept of the Bodhisattva. A bodhisattva is an enlightened being who chooses to return to the earth again and again, to alleviate the suffering of others. Campbell talked about the bodhisattva in the previous chapter. The Buddhist goddess Kuan Yin is one example. Jesus Christ is another. Jesus Christ willingly died on the cross, Campbell says, out of love for us, the world, and God. All of it, the earthly and the heavenly. Viewed this way, "God is love" means that love is *in* everything and *is* everything: the good, bad, and the ugly.

Spiritual love and unrefined forms of passion such as lust share an important characteristic, Campbell says. They are general forms of love that can be expressed toward any number of people. They are impersonal. Compassion, for example, is the ability to care about all suffering, even the suffering of strangers. This is not love for an individual, Campbell says. There is a third type of love, a love that is profound, transformative, and personal. Called *amor*, this concept of love developed from the songs of

"We can safely say, therefore, that
whereas some moralists may find
it possible to make a distinction
between two spheres and reigns—one
of flesh, the other of spirit, one of
time, the other of eternity—wherever
love arises such definitions vanish,
and a sense of life awakens in which
all such oppositions are at one."

—MYTHS TO LIVE BY, *page 154*

"*Love as* passion; *love as* compassion: these are the two extreme poles of our subject. They have been often represented as absolutely opposed—physical, respectively, and spiritual; yet in both the individual is torn out of himself and opened to an experience of rediscovered identity in a larger, more abiding format."

—MYTHS TO LIVE BY, *page 155-56*

the troubadours and Minnesingers in Europe in the twelfth and thirteenth centuries.

As Campbell explains, *amor* was something new. In Medieval Europe, marriage was a matter of politics, economics, social status, or necessity. Love wasn't part of the arrangement. But in the poems and songs about *amor*, people fell in love by choice. This love involved your entire being, the eyes and heart, body and spirit. *Amor* united the physical with the spiritual. Your love for a specific person inspired you to be a better person. You probably recognize *amor* as a shared ideal today, one that defines our expectations of love and our freedom to love whomever we chose.

The freedom to love is an important freedom. We saw this in Medieval Europe, Campbell explains, in the tension between honor and love. Would you take the path of honor and do what others expected, play your assigned role? Or would you follow your heart? Is there a way to do both? These questions are important in the evolution of the European concept of the individual. Campbell turns to the legend of *Parzival* and the Holy Grail by Wolfram von Eschenbach. *Parzival*, he says, is "a monument to the world-saving power of love in all its forms."[1] See a short discussion of *Parzival* in the Points of Interest section below.

Love doesn't necessarily (or even!) bring happiness, Campbell says, but it can be bliss. Love can be a kind of hell and still be your proper place. Bliss is doing what you are meant to do and being fully, authentically yourself. However difficult, that love may be your bliss. It may be your path beyond your small self and small concerns. In fact, Campbell says, what is loveable about a person is the imperfections. Our imperfections are our individuality. They make us unique, and that is what inspires *amor*, a deep personal love for someone special. Perfection inspires admiration, he observes, which is not the same thing.

Throughout *Myths to Live By*, Campbell makes his case for the union of our physical, material existence and our spiritual aspirations. We need to embrace this life and be open to the mystery of the transcendent, he says. Love for an individual, for this experience of body and heart, is profound. It is a path to compassion, to the spiritual love that dissolves all boundaries, even the walls of the separate self. We need to break down the oppositions, he says, and grasp the full power of love. To do this, we need to see Oneness through the eyes of a mystic and at the same time, remember the individual who enters the experience, embraces it, and is dissolved in it. Fully experienced, love will transform you.

Points of Interest

Campbell often told the story of Parzival, the Fisher King, and the Grail. In this instance, he begins with the image of the wasteland. In a wasteland, the powerful don't earn their privilege. People are expected to obey the rules without question. According to Campbell, European societies were a wasteland at the time this story was written. They were dominated by anointed kings and a corrupt Christian church. In the story of Parzival, this wasteland is symbolized by the wounded Grail King, Anfortas, who has not earned his throne. The Fisher King's wound is to his genitals, which represents an unhealthy split between spirit and nature.

The knight Parzival is called to heal this split and restore the health of the kingdom. But first, he has to heal the wasteland in

"*For love is exactly as strong as life. When life produces what the intellect names evil, we may enter into righteous battle, contending 'from loyalty of heart': however, if the principle of love (Christ's 'Love your enemies!') is lost, our humanity too will be lost.*"

—MYTHS TO LIVE BY, *page 168*

himself. He must learn the skills of knighthood and become a loving husband and compassionate man. He must develop good character. He must learn to be himself and to trust his own authority. Parzival fails when he meets King Anfortas because he stifles his own instincts and follows the advice of others. After years of effort and solitary travel, Parzival succeeds. He realizes that his enemy is actually his brother and then heals the kingdom. Love is all. This is Campbell's vision of the hero: a person who does the difficult inner work to become someone who can bring renewal and new life to the community.

COMPLEMENTARY READING FROM CAMPBELL'S WORK

Campbell, Joseph. *The Masks of God, Volume 4: Creative Mythology.* Penguin Books, 1992. *The Collected Works of Joseph Campbell.*

—. *Romance of the Grail: The Magic and Mystery of Arthurian Myth.* Edited by Evans Lansing. New World Library, 2015. *The Collected Works of Joseph Campbell.*

AUDIO RECORDINGS OF CAMPBELL LECTURES

Campbell, Joseph. "The Mythology of Love." Audio Lecture I.6.2. *The Collected Works of Joseph Campbell.*

—. "The Grail Legend." Audio Lecture I.6.4. *The Collected Works of Joseph Campbell.*

FURTHER READING

The Romance of Tristan and Iseult. Retold by J. Bédier. Translated by Hilaire Belloc. Dover Publications, 2005.

Smith, Evans Lansing. *Sacred Mysteries: Myths About Couples in Quest.* Blue Dolphin Publishing, 2003.

Von Eschenbach, Wolfram. *Parzival, A Romance of the Middle Ages.* Translated by Helen M. Mustard and Charles E. Passage. Vintage Books, 1961.

DISCUSSION QUESTIONS

- Reflect on your deepest experience of love. How did/ does this love inspire you to be a better person? Did/ does this love cause you any suffering?

- Campbell says that spiritual forms of love (like compassion) are not inherently greater than "love as passion." Do you agree? What type of love is most difficult for you to offer? To receive?

- Where have you gotten your ideas about love? Does this chapter change those ideas at all?

CREATIVE PROMPTS

- Write a poem about the experience of being in love.
- Make a Valentine.

NOTES

1 Campbell, *Myths to Live By*, 166.

CHAPTER 9
MYTHOLOGIES OF WAR AND PEACE

CHAPTER SUMMARY

"Life lives on life, eats life, and would otherwise not exist."[1]

We all need to eat. Killing and death are part of life, Campbell says, and so it seems, is war. Successful societies have accepted this fact. The need to embrace all of life and enter into the mysterious relationship between life and death is a central theme throughout this book. Again, Campbell urges us in this direction. But is killing in war the same as our biological need to eat? How are these different types of killing and death related? Should we be pessimistic about the prospect of a peaceful human community? What do our myths tell us about these questions?

According to Campbell, there are two different mythologies about the act of killing. In one mythology, the necessity of death and killing is totally accepted. Killing is a powerful, life-affirming act. Campbell puts indigenous cultures in this group. He notes that farmers as well as hunters ritualized killing and sacrifice in service to life. The decaying bodies of plants that fertilize new growth, like the carcasses of animals, make clear the connection between life and death. Indigenous cultures also accept conflict and war as part of the brutal truth of life.

In Campbell's other mythology, killing and war are seen as necessary evils. These acts are acceptable only under the right conditions. In the ideal world of these mythologies, war would not exist. Conflict is a resolvable moral issue, not a fact of life.

Campbell says this second group is romantic, reform oriented, and doomed to failure. These cultures and their myths haven't achieved peace, he says, and they never will, because they remain outside the mysteries of life and death. Somehow, visions of peace must exist within the reality of "life feeds on life."

Campbell highlights an important difference between these two mythologies, beyond their belief in the prospect of peace. In cultures with a life- and death-affirming mythology, one that accepts killing and war, the victims and enemies are honored along with the warriors and heroes. The losers matter as much as the winners. In cultures that put conditions on killing and see war as evil, there is no honor given to victims and enemies. Campbell turns to "the two great Western war myths"—the ancient Greek *Iliad* and the Hebrew Bible—to explain this point.

At the time these two myths emerged, he says, people had imagined gods in their own, human image. The god was not imagined in the form of a bear, for example. These are myths of war, not hunting. In both of these myths, humanlike gods or God decide when and how a war should be fought. In the *Iliad*, the Greek gods create the conflict that begins the Trojan War. The gods fight among themselves, and so they make people fight. The gods have champions on both sides, like fans of opposing football teams. Some of the Greek gods and goddesses support the Greeks and their heroes. Some of them support the Trojans and heroes of Troy. The gods are actively involved. Both sides want the honor of winning. The gods also want sacrifice and worship. After ten years, the Greeks win.

The *Iliad*, Campbell observes, was written for the victorious Greeks. It is their story, and yet much of the poem is dedicated

"It is for an obvious reason far easier to name examples of mythologies of war than mythologies of peace; for not only has conflict between groups been normal to human experience, but there is also the cruel fact to be recognized that killing is the precondition of all living whatsoever: life lives on life, eats life, and would otherwise not exist."

—MYTHS TO LIVE BY, *page 169*

to honoring their enemy, the Trojans. The Trojan hero Hector, for example, is considered the most admirable warrior by both sides. This honoring of the enemy is also found in ancient Greek plays about the Trojan War and other wars fought by the Greeks. The Greeks believed that war is inevitable because the gods will it to happen, even if humans don't want to fight. We're all in this world with war and death together, bound by the same laws of life. War is tragic for every human being whose life is touched by it.

In the Hebrew Bible, God tells the Israelites to wage war for their glory and his own. The spoils of war are God's bounty, gifted to the people of Israel. Once again, war is divinely inspired and the hero fights with "God" on his side. There is an important difference though. In this mythology there is only one God. There is only one side that deserves to win. God tells the Israelites to utterly destroy their enemies. They are all inferior or bad people who deserve to die or become slaves. In this view, war is not inevitable. War is a means to God's peace. Peace will come when the Israelites rule over everyone else, and when all of them are properly subservient to God.

Campbell reminds us that Islam springs from this same mythological tradition. He draws a parallel between the Christian Crusades and the Islamic jihad. Judaism, Christianity, and Islam draw from related myths. These religions share foundational stories and prophetic figures. Despite this common heritage, Muslims, Jews, and Christians have fought and killed each other for centuries, Campbell says. The conflict continues to this day because each believes they are *the* chosen people of the one God.

Campbell discusses the biblical roots of the Middle Eastern conflict at some length. He concludes with the message of peace delivered in the teachings of Jesus. What happened to "turn the other cheek"? Jesus urged his followers to cultivate peace in their own hearts, Campbell says, and unite with the god within. Early Christianity was a mystical religion. Like Buddhism, Christianity involved renouncing and withdrawing from the world to fight the battles in your own heart and mind. These mystical Christian teachings are difficult and have never been mainstream. The desire for peace gained through a great holy war has not diminished. There is also a problem, Campbell suggests, with extreme asceticism and withdrawal from the world. When you give up on the physical life of the body, you risk giving up the will to live. Do we want to die in order to be peaceful and do no harm?

What is found in Asian mythologies of war and peace? Peace has been unattainable in these cultures too, Campbell observes. Buddhism seems to offer a solution. Here the path to peace is psychological. The conflict is within you. The goal is to quench ego, Campbell says, not life. And yet the pursuit of virtue can become a denial of life, dependent on withdrawing from the world. And is it virtuous, he asks, to be unwilling to defend anyone or anything at all? Like Buddhism, peace in the Taoist tradition is also based on inner harmony and acceptance of the world. In Taoism, there is an essential harmony in all things, contained in the dynamic relationship between yin and yang. Recognize this interplay in your own being and harmonize with the shift and flow of the world.

These are profound ideas, and there has been plenty of war in these cultures, Campbell says. The best summary of Asian thought about war and peace might be found in the Hindu Bhagavad Gita. Through the conversation between the warrior

Arjuna and the god Krishna, we learn that there is no peace in life, in the field of action. It is impossible. The way to attain peace is to do your duty without attachment, to act without expectation. This is possible when you understand that our imperfect world is already perfect. We create opposing categories, dualities like "good" and "evil," but reality exists beyond these. Paradoxically, Campbell says, the mythology of peace and the mythology of war are the same in this instance.

Campbell ends with the mention of a contemporary idea that peace can be based on ethical principles and the rational calculation of mutual advantage. Nations and people will find ways to live peacefully when peace is in the best interest of everyone. This won't be possible, he observes, until every one of us makes the decision to live in peace.

Points of Interest

Campbell talks about a third mythological viewpoint on war and peace, namely that war is inevitable now but peace will reign when God brings the world to an end. Campbell traces this idea to the sixth century BCE and the ascendance of the Aryan Persians. Cyrus the Great built a huge, multicultural empire, Campbell says, based on the mythology of the prophet Zarathustra. According to this myth, war is the result of a cosmic battle between good and evil. The God of Light fights the powers of evil and darkness. God created a perfect world but the earth has fallen into evil and ignorance as the result of this struggle. Each if us must choose to fight on the side of God, goodness, light.

Cyrus the Great was a relatively benevolent ruler. He made the lands that he conquered colonies, for example, rather than killing everyone or exiling them into slavery, which was the common practice. As a result, he was called the "King of Kings" and was seen as God's agent for peace on earth. He waged war to establish peace under his control. This was an early model for the kind of messiah envisioned by the ancient Hebrews.

Over the centuries, many people have believed that violence was justified to establish the benevolent rule of divinely appointed monarchs and political leaders. Many have believed in this cosmic struggle and the wars of the righteous. They have believed that it is better to be killed than to live on the wrong side. This mythology of perfect peace has been a call to perpetual war.

Complementary Reading from Campbell's Work

Campbell, Joseph. *The Masks of God, Volume 4: Creative Mythology.* Penguin Books, 1992. *The Collected Works of Joseph Campbell.*

Zimmer, Heinrich. *The King and the Corpse: Tales of the Soul's Conquest of Evil.* Edited by Joseph Campbell. Princeton University Press, Bollingen Series XI, 1957.

Further Reading

The Bhagavad Gita. Translated by W.J. Johnson. Oxford University Press, 1994.

Homer. *The Iliad*. Translated by Robert Fagles. With introduction and notes by Bernard Knox. Penguin Books, 1990.

Keen, Sam. *Faces of the Enemy: Reflections of the Hostile Imagination*. Harper & Row, 1986.

Miles, Jack. *God, A Biography*. Random House, 1995.

Mitchell, Stephen. *Tao Te Ching, A New English Version*. Harper & Row, 1988.

Sun-Tzu. *The Art of War*. Translated by Thomas Cleary. Shambhala, 1988.

Discussion Questions

- Do you agree with Campbell when he says that war must be accepted because killing is necessary to life? Why or why not?

- Do you strive to be a peaceful person? What does being peaceful mean to you, and how do you achieve it?

- Campbell refers to the ancient Greek philosopher Heraclitus, who said that war is the creator of all great things. Do you think this is true? Why or why not?

- Do you think the possibility of world peace, through the recognition of mutual best interest, is more or less likely in our times? Can human beings live peacefully together?

CREATIVE PROMPTS

- Think of a conflict currently underway in the world. Imagine that you are the chief negotiator and write a speech that you would deliver to both sides of the conflict.

- Your society has fought a war at some point in its history. Write a song that honors the people who were defeated.

NOTES

1 Campbell, *Myths to Live By*, 169.

CHAPTER 10

SCHIZOPHRENIA—THE INWARD JOURNEY

CHAPTER SUMMARY

In this chapter, Campbell further explores the instinctual basis of mythologizing. Earlier, he defined mythology as enduring patterns in the human imagination. He explained the openness of human nature, imprinting, and our need for mythic models. Now he expands these topics to include the work of two clinical psychologists: Dr. John Perry and Dr. Stanislav Grof. Perry researched schizophrenia; Grof was researching the therapeutic use of LSD. Campbell also returns to C.G. Jung's theories about psychology and myth. This research into human psychology confirms our mythological instinct, Campbell says. The mythological hero, shaman, mystic, LSD traveler, and schizophrenic go on similar inward journeys.

Just as the physical body inherits patterns of behavior, human consciousness inherits patterns of thought and meaning. C.G. Jung called these patterns archetypes. Jung developed his theory based on the dreams and artwork of his clients, which had mythological roots well outside the individual's personal experience. Mythic material can deeply affect us. Campbell has talked about mythic images and living symbols. Now he calls them "energy-evoking and -directing" signs.[1] Body and consciousness are not isolated from one another. Mythology is like a biological organ, Campbell explains. It speaks to the nervous system.

We are born with the instinct *for* myth but not *with* a myth. Mythic symbols arise naturally in our consciousness but we construct meaning and myth from them. We are imprinted, Campbell says, with the mythology of our family and society. This mythology must fit our lived experience. A properly functioning myth will provide meaning and guidance. It will connect us to the world and to our community. Campbell discusses the four functions of mythology that I reviewed in the Points of Interest section in Chapter 3. Today, however, many people do not have a functioning myth. They don't have a myth to live by.

A person can lose their mythic ground in a number of ways: Bad imprinting. Major changes in the outside world. Challenges in the inner life. When this happens, you don't feel at home in the world. You don't feel connected to society or even to your innermost self. This disorientation can have disastrous consequences for everyone. It can become a crisis. One extreme form of the crisis is schizophrenia. Another form of crisis is terror and despair in the face of death, serious illness, or other major life challenges.

How do you navigate this situation and avoid a serious problem? When you look at the shamanic experience, Campbell says, you find that shamans make a similar inward journey into mythic realms. Shamanism is a deep dive, often spontaneous, into the deep waters of the unconscious psyche. The similarity in images and experience is further proof, he says, that the source of our myths is instinctual or archetypal. The shamanic experience can also help us understand other forms of the journey, and how to survive them when they become a crisis.

The shaman has the context and support that are necessary for the journey. The community understands and honors the experience as meaningful. The shaman has a "mental breakdown"

"The mystic, endowed with native talents for this sort of thing and following, stage by stage, the instruction of a master, enters the waters and finds he can swim; whereas the schizophrenic, unprepared, unguided, and ungifted, has fallen or has intentionally plunged, and is drowning."

—MYTHS TO LIVE BY, *page 209*

but it is considered a gift. Campbell describes the initiation of an Eskimo shaman, as related by the Danish explorer Knud Rasmussen. In European cultures, a spontaneous break with outer reality is considered a serious illness without any positive value. Dr. Perry, Dr. Grof, and Jung before them, were curious and brave enough to explore psychotic experiences, so this attitude can change.

The shape of these journeys into the unconscious realms of myth follows the pattern that Campbell calls the "hero journey."[2] The hero's journey involves three stages: separation from the familiar world, a dangerous and difficult initiation, and a return to the world to serve others. The hero is transformed by this journey. One example in Greek mythology is the journey of Odysseus. See the Points of Interest section below for more details. Campbell offers detailed descriptions of the stages in a psychotic break and LSD trip that sound markedly similar. So does Dr. Stanislav Grof's rebirthing work. In reliving their birth experience, people pass through stages that are painful and frightening, release emotional baggage, and find a state of transpersonal ecstasy.

This ecstasy, the direct, personal realization of the underlying unity of the cosmos, is the culmination of the journey. It is the awakening described in myths from around the world.

Each of us needs to make an inward journey. We don't all achieve enlightenment and yet we must survive a second birth into adulthood. Those of us called to do so must complete the passage to our mature individuality, or individuation. A meaningful mythological context and support can guide us through rough waters without shipwreck. A living symbol can inspire our true character and help us develop inner authority. It can lead us to the deepest truth of existence and our own being.

Points of Interest

Campbell draws parallels between a range of intense psychological experiences and the mythological pattern of the hero's journey. The key to your return home, Campbell says, is that you never identify with the figures and powers that you meet. You must hold onto your awareness of your self to complete the journey.

He turns to Homer's *Odyssey* to provide a mythic example. Odysseus, an ancient Greek hero, attempts to sail home to Ithaca after the Trojan War. The gods blow him off course. For twenty years, Odysseus wanders and suffers in strange and dangerous lands. Campbell describes this as an inward journey. Odysseus wasn't fit to go back to domestic life until he was initiated by the archetypal feminine. He meets this powerful force in three different forms.

There is no guarantee that Odysseus will survive this ordeal. He meets many forms of danger: monsters, goddesses, nymphs, whirlpools, gods. All of them are deadly because they threaten to erase his desire to return home, through death, drugs, or seduction. His desire for Ithaca and his wife, Penelope, is the thread that keeps him connected to his known world and identity. Odysseus is transformed by his experience, and he manages to complete the process because he never forgets his familiar world, his home.

"The ultimate aim of the quest, if one is to return, must be neither release or ecstasy for oneself, but the wisdom and power to serve others."

—MYTHS TO LIVE BY, *page 227*

Complementary Reading from Campbell's Work

Campbell, Joseph. *The Hero with a Thousand Faces*. Bollingen Series xvii. Third edition. New World Library, 2008. *The Collected Works of Joseph Campbell.*

——. *The Masks of God, Volume 1: Primitive Mythology*. Edited by David Kudler. New World Library, 2020. *The Collected Works of Joseph Campbell.*

——. *A Joseph Campbell Companion: Reflections on the Art of Living*. Edited by Diane K. Osbon. Harper Perennial, 1995.

Audio Recordings of Campbell Lectures

Campbell, Joseph. "The Inward Journey." Audio Lecture I.2.2. *The Collected Works of Joseph Campbell.*

——. "The Thresholds of Mythology." Audio Lecture I.2.1. *The Collected Works of Joseph Campbell.*

——. "Personal Myth." Audio Lecture I.4.5. *The Collected Works of Joseph Campbell.*

——. "Psychosis and the Hero's Journey." Audio Lecture II.2.3. *The Collected Works of Joseph Campbell.*

Further Reading

Davis, Wade. *The Wayfinders: Why Ancient Wisdom Matters in the Modern World*. House of Anansi Press, 2009.

"The inward journeys of the mythical hero, the shaman, the mystic, and the schizophrenic are in principle the same; and when the return or remission occurs, it is experienced as a rebirth: the birth, that is to say, of a 'twice-born' ego, no longer bound by its daylight-world horizon."

—MYTHS TO LIVE BY, *page 230*

Grof, Stanislav. *The Cosmic Game: Explorations of the Frontiers of Human Consciousness*. State University of New York Press; illustrated edition, 1998.

Halifax, Joan. *Shaman: The Wounded Healer*. Thames & Hudson, 1988.

Laing, R.D. *The Politics of Experience*. Pantheon, 1983.

Discussion Questions

- Where do you see mythological imprinting in your life? How have the myths of your family and society shaped you and your values? Your lifestyle?

- Where do you see the pattern of the hero's journey in your life? How did this experience transform you?

- Are you in need of a new myth to live by? Why or why not?

Creative Prompts

- Write a story that reveals your family's mythology and describes how it was handed down to you.

- Make a painting or collage of your inner journey.

- Write a poem about the moment you understood something important about your life.

NOTES

1 Campbell, *Myths to Live By*, 213.
2 Ibid, 202.

CHAPTER II
THE MOON WALK—
THE OUTWARD JOURNEY

CHAPTER SUMMARY

On July 20, 1969, human beings walked on the moon for the first time. According to Campbell, this awesome accomplishment has mythological importance for the whole world. Mythology has become fact, he says. How many of us have fully grasped this? That we could, while here on earth, make the mathematical calculations about space that were necessary to succeed confirms the ancient mythological insight. We do carry the laws of the cosmos within us. We are creatures of space and time. The outward journey and the inner journey are one and the same.

We also have a powerful new image, the breathtakingly beautiful photograph of planet earth, as viewed from outer space. This awe-inspiring image can support the new mythology of a global community and a world "with no horizons," Campbell says.

The moon is over two hundred thousand miles away from earth. Until Neil Armstrong and his colleagues left tracks in the moon dust, the moon was primarily a mythic figure. Our knowledge of the moon was based on what we could see from earth, and what we could imagine. This changed, Campbell says, with Copernicus. Copernicus proposed a mathematical model of the universe. Later, Newton added to it. This knowledge was abstract. It was based in the mind, not what you could see with your eyes. Through watching the space flight and the moon walk, Campbell explains, we now see abstract math in action.

"Now there is a telling image: this earth, the one oasis in all space, an extraordinary kind of sacred grove, as it were, set apart for the rituals of life; and not simply one part or section of this earth, but the entire globe now a sanctuary, a set-apart Blessed Place."

—MYTHS TO LIVE BY, *page 237*

The invisible and visible unite. The moon of the mind and the moon of the eyes have come together.

What will be required for us to understand the profundity of the moon walk and the possibilities it offers us? Curiosity will get us started. Wonder at our discoveries will drive us further. Awe takes us beyond the mundane concerns of economics, politics, or entertainment, Campbell says. He points to the mysterious slab in the mythic movie *2001: A Space Odyssey*. The slab is a metaphor for the unknown, he says. What drives human evolution in the movie and in life are curiosity and fascination with the mystery. The greatest human accomplishments are inspired by awe.

Our domestication of fire is one example, he says. We are the only animals who have learned to use fire. Why did we do this? Because fire is fascinating. Fire inspires awe. The practical uses of fire have been instrumental in human evolution, he explains, but it must have been the mysterious power of fire that first attracted our ancestors. Fire transforms everything. There's nothing else like it. We also see an aspect of self in fire, Campbell says. We have an inner fire. We generate heat. We grow by combining fuel and oxygen.

Humans have seen themselves, he says, in everything they have revered and mythologized. Many aspects of this world have fascinated us. We can make a life around any of them, Campbell explains, because our nature is open. We learn to be human. Our ancestors found awe and wonder in the lives of animals and plants, and the movement of the celestial bodies. They created mythologies and formed living symbols from these sources. What will provide this for us now?

We have moved past the models for life that these images inspired, Campbell says, and our concept of the individual has changed. Now we have the idea of a unique person who is valued as such, and expected to bring something into the world. Maybe the human being will be the source of awe. Maybe we will see ourselves as we are: a microcosm of the whole, the eyes and ears of an intelligent earth. Campbell shares an anecdote about Alan Watts, an American Buddhist and poet, who famously said that the earth "peoples" just as an apple tree "apples." See the Points of Interest section below for more about Alan Watts and this idea.

Science, as Campbell discusses in the opening chapter of *Myths to Live By*, has long been seen as the enemy of myth. Now we have a science, with the moon walk as a brilliant demonstration, that supports the most profound mythological truth. The microcosm of our own being, of our body and consciousness, is analogous with the cosmos. Everything is One, and the All is in everything.

What new myth will arise from this discovery? What can lure us beyond what we think we can do to a new state of being? The human capacity for awe and our unflagging curiosity, Campbell says, will be the key to that discovery.

POINTS OF INTEREST

Alan Watts proposed an alternative to the Christian mythology. Christians see the earth as a created place where they were sent for a limited time. They are merely visitors here and Heaven is their true home. But isn't the earth your source? Humans are part of the earth and comprised of the same elements. This is where we are born, grow, and die. Our lives are dependent on the earth. You come *out* of the earth, Watts said, not *into* the earth.

This understanding of earth as source also changes your view of the earth. If humans are intelligent, the earth must be intelligent. We couldn't evolve independent from our source.

COMPLEMENTARY READING FROM CAMPBELL'S WORK

Campbell, Joseph. *The Inner Reaches of Outer Space: Metaphor as Myth and as Religion.* New World Library, 2012. *The Collected Works of Joseph Campbell.*

AUDIO RECORDINGS OF CAMPBELL LECTURES

Campbell, Joseph. "Experiencing the Divine" Audio Lecture I.5.3. *The Collected Works of Joseph Campbell.*

—. "Mythologies New, Old & Today." Audio Lecture II.5.1. *The Collected Works of Joseph Campbell.*

"There are no laws out there that are not right here; no gods out there that are not right here, and not only here, but within us, in our minds."

—MYTHS TO LIVE BY, *page 244*

"We are at this moment participating in one of the very greatest leaps of the human spirit to a knowledge not only of outside nature but also of our own deep inward mystery that has ever been taken, or that ever will or ever can be taken."

—MYTHS TO LIVE BY, *page 247*

FURTHER READING

Fetter-Vorm, Jonathan. *Moonbound: Apollo 11 and the Dream of Spaceflight*. Foreword by Michael Collins. Hill and Wang, 2019.

Schrodinger, Erwin. *My View of the World*. Cambridge University Press, 1964.

Watts, Alan W. "Western Mythology: Its Dissolution and Transformation." *Myths, Dreams, and Religions: Eleven Visions of Connection*. Edited by Joseph Campbell. E.P. Dutton, 1970.

DISCUSSION QUESTIONS

- I encourage you to watch the Apollo 11 moon walk by Armstrong and Aldrin. If it's been years since you've seen it, you might want to watch it again. How do Campbell's insights affect your experience?

- What do you think Campbell might say about the current state of space travel and plans for human colonies on the moon and beyond?

- How do you feel about Campbell's assessment of personal freedom and secular society? Do you think he was right, or was his evaluation premature? Has society gone backward? Forward?

- Does the photograph of the earth from space inspire awe in you? Why or why not?

CREATIVE PROMPTS

- Find an image of something in the material world that fills you with awe. Write about the ways in which you are similar. If this image is a metaphor for your own being, what does it express?

- Make a list of changes that have taken place in your lifetime that you didn't imagine were possible.

- Write a short science fiction about something that hasn't happened yet, but could.

CHAPTER 12
ENVOY: NO MORE HORIZONS

CHAPTER SUMMARY

Campbell has led us through an amazing range of ideas. In the final chapter, he touches on his central points. He sketches his vision of a world with no more horizons, and encourages each of us to find our myth to live by.

Mythology is the story of our inner journey, he reminds us, not history or material facts. Mythic images, like dreams, come from the psyche and tell us about the psyche. Myth is a symbolic language, a vocabulary of images that must be read metaphorically. When you approach myths this way, you discover that myths from all cultures point to the same truth: Thou Art That. The mystery of our being is the mystery of the cosmos. God is found within. The All is the One and the One is All. God is in everything else too. The eternal is discovered and lived in the present. Aldous Huxley called this "the perennial philosophy."

Differences in mythologies have created conflict between people because their symbols weren't read as metaphors. Centuries of doctrine and dogma compound the problem. In the past, conflict could be avoided by physically separating. Today, this isn't possible. Our sheer numbers and our technologies bring us together. Cultures collide. Paradigms meet. Modern science meets the archaic. Everything is coming together for the first time, in a new way. This naturally causes conflict and turmoil,

"What gods are there, what gods have there ever been, that were not from man's imagination? We know their histories: we know by what stages they developed."

—MYTHS TO LIVE BY, *page 253*

Campbell says. That's part of the process. It's time for us to sift through the contents of our old paradigms, to preserve the wisdom that we still need and discard the rest. It's time to create one human community on planet earth.

When you understand the universal message in our myths, you see our shared aspirations and challenges. The gods are projections of our psyche, created from patterns in the human imagination. We hold their truths in common. At the same time, the European concept of the individual gives us a revolutionary level of freedom and responsibility. There is no authority and no doctrine that can claim absolute truth or superiority anymore. Our myths tell us about the god within. Each of us is a microcosm of the whole and the center of our own experience. We must find our own path to self-realization. In this world of "no more horizons," there are no boundaries around our imagination or limits to our possibilities.

The first step is to regain a sense of wonder. Wonder at the natural world. At the cosmos. At the mystery of life. At the dimensions of your own being. The first and central function of myth today is to "cleanse the doors of perception," as Aldous Huxley says, and restore a sense of wonder. Science can connect us to wonder in harmony with mythic truth. The moon walk demonstrated that we are indeed a microcosm of the cosmos. This has been the message of all mythologies. We now know definitively that we are the eyes and ears and mind of the earth and of the universe, Campbell says. This is the discovery of the outward journey.

The science of the inward journey, like Grof's research into LSD, is also a path to wonder. Like the moon walk, this is scientific evidence that mythology is psychological, and that our psychology is part of the larger consciousness of the cosmos. People who travel the deeper levels of consciousness, into the unconscious, have experiences described in our myths. You'll find more about Grof's LSD research in the Points of Interest section below.

These scientific breakthroughs about the outward and inward journeys support a new mythology of the perennial philosophy. Campbell talks about Huxley's psychotropic drug experiences and what they reveal. In an ordinary state of consciousness, our brain and nervous system selectively filter sensory stimuli from the world. We only process what we need to survive, otherwise our ego-consciousness would be overwhelmed. Our awareness shrinks to support our animal survival but there's so much more. Huxley calls this the "Mind at Large."[1]

In non-ordinary states of consciousness, like the one induced by certain drugs, you temporarily bypass the filters. You contact the Mind at Large. You can apprehend and handle more of reality, Huxley says. You still can't get all of it, but there's much more and it's different. The process of achieving this state of consciousness, or your degree of openness to the Mind at Large, is the topic of mythology Campbell explains. We have stories about people who were born with easy access to Mind at Large, and stories about how to achieve it.

The beautiful image of the earth, floating in space, is concrete and inspiring proof that we are all one community, the eyes and ears of a shared planet. In his final pages, Campbell asks us once again, "What is—or what is to be—the new mythology?"[2]

"*The first condition, therefore, that any mythology must fulfill if it is to render life to modern lives is that of cleansing the doors of perception to the wonder, at once terrible and fascinating, of ourselves and of the universe of which we are the ears and eyes and the mind.*"

—MYTHS TO LIVE BY, *page 257*

POINTS OF INTEREST

As Stanislav Grof discovered, the stages of an LSD experience contain mythic material and mirror mythological journeys. The first stages typically involve an expansion of sensory and bodily powers and bring the ability to see and hear with greater sensitivity. As you move deeper into the experience, you make a dive into your personal unconscious. You have the opportunity to relive past events and sort emotional baggage in a useful way.

You may go back in your life to relive your birth experience. Most of this experience is terrifying. You see yourself as a passive victim and as a violent aggressor. You battle monsters and face horrors like those described in a mythic hero's journey. The process ends with a release into ecstasy. Images from Asian traditions often appear in the final rebirth experience of cosmic oneness and bliss. This ego death and awareness of the transpersonal is mythological, Campbell explains. Your personal suffering becomes the collective suffering of all, and then radiant love for all. You are the center of being, the Source.

COMPLEMENTARY READING FROM CAMPBELL'S WORK

Campbell, Joseph. *The Flight of the Wild Gander: Explorations in the Mythological Dimensions, Selected Essays 1944–1968.* New World Library, 2018. *The Collected Works of Joseph Campbell.*

—. *The Mythic Dimension, Selected Essays 1959–1987.* Edited by Antony Van Couvering. New World Library, 2007. *The Collected Works of Joseph Campbell.*

AUDIO RECORDINGS OF CAMPBELL LECTURES

Campbell, Joseph. "Mythic Themes in Literature and Art." Audio Lecture II.2.1. *The Collected Works of Joseph Campbell.*

—. "Birth of the Perennial Mythology." Audio: Lecture II.1.9. *The Collected Works of Joseph Campbell.*

FURTHER READING

Huxley, Aldous. *The Perennial Philosophy.* Harper Perennial Modern Classics, 2009.

Smith, Huston. *Beyond the Postmodern Mind.* Third edition. Quest Books, 2003.

DISCUSSION QUESTIONS

- How have Campbell's ideas changed the way that you understand mythology?

- Campbell wrote *Myths to Live By* in 1972. Do you see evidence of his impact on the world? What form does this take?

- Has he influenced European culture in particular? How?

- What do you think about a world with no horizons? Do you share Campbell's vision?

- Do you have a myth to live by? If so, what is it, and how does it guide you? If not, why not?

"We can no longer hold our loves at home and project our aggressions elsewhere; for on this spaceship Earth there is no 'elsewhere' anymore. And no mythology that continues to speak of 'elsewheres' and 'outsiders' meets the requirements of this hour."

—MYTHS TO LIVE BY, *page 226*

CREATIVE PROMPTS

- Write about what you've discovered about the role of mythology in your life.

- Write a poem inspired by the Mind at Large.

NOTES

1 Campbell, *Myths to Live By*, 263.
2 Ibid, 266.

Final Thoughts from
Catherine Svehla, PhD

Writing this skeleton key for you has been a wonderful opportunity to make a deep dive into this incredible book. It has also been a challenge. Distilling and synthesizing the many ideas that Campbell presents wasn't easy. I hope that I've succeeded in creating a useful key, one that unlocks the many treasures in these pages and inspires you to explore Campbell's other work. Before we part ways, I'd like to share a new understanding that emerged for me while writing this guide.

When I first encountered Campbell, many years ago, he spoke to the imaginative part of my being. To the artist and mystic in me. Campbell's scholarship and passion for mythology validated my yearning for what mythology offered: images and poetic metaphors, compelling characters, mystery and meaning that fed my soul. I loved the mythic hero's journey as a model for psychological growth and spiritual awakening. I still do.

What I didn't notice was Campbell's insistence that science must play a role in the formation of our new mythologies. I was focused on the instruction to read myths metaphorically, in order to find common meanings. The idea that mythology could bridge cultural mythological divides was exciting. And yet the conflict between the world view of science and that of mythology felt irreconcilable. I've always loved Campbell's story of the boy and his mother at the lunch counter in Chapter 1. I find his analysis illuminating. But I didn't see how science could offer a useful link between the inner journey and the outer world.

Revisiting this work today, I'm struck by the connection between our scientific understanding of the material world and our myth-making. This is embedded in Campbell's historical accounts of our evolving mythologies. He provides this historical background in Chapters 1, 2, 4, and 11. Shifts from one mythic framework to another occur as knowledge of the visible world changes. Our outer life experience provides the images and metaphors that give rise to the theories and theologies that describe our inner journey. The scientific and the mythic meet in our imagination.

Before my work on this Skeleton Key Study Guide, I viewed science as a mechanistic, reductive, abstract, and unfeeling approach to the world. Now I understand that science can be more than an obstacle to literal belief in the old myths. As a result, I've started reading books written by scientists like Alan Lightman and Hope Jahren, who share their wonderment at our extraordinary cosmos. I've found scientists who weave mythology into their work, like Robin Wall Kimmerer, author of *Braiding Sweetgrass*. I've also found fiction writers weaving new science into their stories. *The Overstory* by Richard Powers, for example, is a novel about the shared evolution and need for partnership between humans and trees.

Scientific knowledge provides metaphors that can shape new myths. It can also usher in experiences of wonder and awe that inspire us to go beyond our assumed limitations. As a mythologist, I'm intrigued by what science will contribute to our changing mythologies. Personally, I'm curious about where this new avenue of discovery may take me. According to Campbell, awe at the mysteries of existence leads us to locate those mysteries in our own being. Campbell found inspiration in the photograph of planet earth taken by the crew of Apollo 11. This fed his sense of the possible. What might provide this for me? For you?

I've turned to *Myths to Live By* numerous times over the years. I find a new and exciting detail, idea, or theme every time. I hope the time that you've spent with *Myths to Live By* has deepened your understanding of mythology and inspires you to live your mythic adventure. May it be creative, fulfilling, and full of wonder.

ABOUT JOSEPH CAMPBELL

Joseph Campbell was an American author and teacher best known for his work in the field of comparative mythology. He was born in New York City in 1904, and from early childhood he became interested in mythology. He loved to read books about Indigenous American cultures, and frequently visited the American Museum of Natural History in New York, where he was fascinated by the museum's collection of totem poles. Campbell was educated at Columbia University, where he specialized in medieval literature, and, after earning a master's degree, continued his studies at universities in Paris and Munich. While abroad he was influenced by the art of Pablo Picasso and Henri Matisse, the novels of James Joyce and Thomas Mann, and the psychological studies of Sigmund Freud and Carl Jung. These encounters led to Campbell's theory that all myths and epics are linked in the human psyche, and that they are cultural manifestations of the need to explain social, cosmological, and spiritual realities.

After a period in California, where he encountered John Steinbeck and the biologist Ed Ricketts, Campbell taught at the Canterbury School, and then, in 1934, joined the literature department at Sarah Lawrence College, a post he retained for many years. During the 1940s and '50s, he helped Swami Nikhilananda to translate the Upaniṣads and *The Gospel of Sri Ramakrishna*. He also edited works by the German scholar Heinrich Zimmer on Indian art, myths, and philosophy. In 1944, with Henry Morton Robinson, Campbell published *A Skeleton Key to Finnegans Wake*. His first original work, *The Hero with a Thousand Faces*, came out in 1949 and was immediately well received; in time, it became acclaimed as a classic. In this study of the "myth of the hero," Campbell asserted that there is a single pattern of heroic journey and that all cultures share this essential pattern in their various heroic myths. In his book he also outlined the basic conditions, stages, and results of the archetypal hero's journey.

Joseph Campbell died in 1987. In 1988, a series of television interviews with Bill Moyers, *The Power of Myth*, introduced Campbell's views to millions of people.

About the Author

Catherine Svehla, PhD, is an independent scholar, consultant, and mentor in the mythic life. She works with artists and creative individuals who want to apply a mythic and archetypal lens to life and work, and offers thought-provoking story circles, workshops, and other mythic tools to open the imagination. Catherine is the host of the Myth Matters podcast, an exploration of myth in contemporary life, and a member of the Joseph Campbell Foundation's MythMaker℠ Podcast Network. A recognized innovator in the field of mythological studies, Catherine received a New Mythos grant from OPUS Archives.

Learn more about Catherine's work at mythicmojo.com.

ABOUT THE JOSEPH CAMPBELL FOUNDATION

The Joseph Campbell Foundation invites you to experience the power of myth. Building on the work of Joseph Campbell, we offer resources and community for those who hear the call to adventure.

For more information about Joseph Campbell and the Joseph Campbell Foundation, contact:

Joseph Campbell Foundation
www.jcf.org

CPSIA information can be obtained
at www.ICGtesting.com
Printed in the USA
JSHW070726070723
44277JS00006B/15